797,885 Books

are available to read at

www.ForgottenBooks.com

Forgotten Books' App
Available for mobile, tablet & eReader

ISBN 978-1-331-52550-9
PIBN 10105505

This book is a reproduction of an important historical work. Forgotten Books uses
state-of-the-art technology to digitally reconstruct the work, preserving the original format
whilst repairing imperfections present in the aged copy. In rare cases, an imperfection in
the original, such as a blemish or missing page, may be replicated in our edition. We do,
however, repair the vast majority of imperfections successfully; any imperfections that
remain are intentionally left to preserve the state of such historical works.

Forgotten Books is a registered trademark of FB &c Ltd.
Copyright © 2015 FB &c Ltd.
FB &c Ltd, Dalton House, 60 Windsor Avenue, London, SW19 2RR.
Company number 08720141. Registered in England and Wales.

For support please visit www.forgottenbooks.com

1 MONTH OF
FREE
READING

at
www.ForgottenBooks.com

By purchasing this book you are eligible for one month membership to ForgottenBooks.com, giving you unlimited access to our entire collection of over 700,000 titles via our web site and mobile apps.

To claim your free month visit:
www.forgottenbooks.com/free105505

* Offer is valid for 45 days from date of purchase. Terms and conditions apply.

English
Français
Deutsche
Italiano
Español
Português

www.forgottenbooks.com

Mythology Photography **Fiction**
Fishing Christianity **Art** Cooking
Essays Buddhism Freemasonry
Medicine **Biology** Music **Ancient**
Egypt Evolution Carpentry Physics
Dance Geology **Mathematics** Fitness
Shakespeare **Folklore** Yoga Marketing
Confidence Immortality Biographies
Poetry **Psychology** Witchcraft
Electronics Chemistry History **Law**
Accounting **Philosophy** Anthropology
Alchemy Drama Quantum Mechanics
Atheism Sexual Health **Ancient History**
Entrepreneurship Languages Sport
Paleontology Needlework Islam
Metaphysics Investment Archaeology
Parenting Statistics Criminology
Motivational

A·

ITALIA ESPANA

GUÁRDESE COMO

JOYA PRECIOSA

EX-LIBRIS

M. A. BUCHANAN

PRESENTED TO

THE LIBRARY

BY

PROFESSOR MILTON A. BUCHANAN

OF THE

DEPARTMENT OF ITALIAN AND SPANISH

1906-1946

Mariana

IN SAME SERIES.

The Lady from the Sea.

A London Plane Tree, and other Poems.

Iphigenia in Delphi.

Mireio.

Lyrics.

A Minor Poet.

Concerning Cats.

A Chaplet from the Greek Anthology.

The Countess Kathleen.

The Love Songs of Robert Burns.

Love Songs of Ireland.

Retrospect, and other Poems.

Brand.

Son of Don Juan.   By José ECHEGARAY.

A Mr Graham
en prueba de amistad
José Echagaray

JOSÉ ECHEGARAY

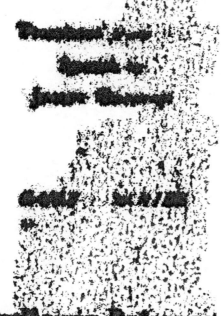

Mariana

AN ORIGINAL DRAMA

In Three Acts and an Epilogue

by

JOSÉ ECHEGARAY

Translated from the
Spanish by
JAMES GRAHAM

CAMEO SERIES

T. Fisher Unwin PaternosterSq.
London E.C. MDCCCXCV.

PQ
6516
M313

PERSONS OF THE DRAMA.

MARIANA, *aged 24 years.*

CLARA, *wife of Don Castulo,* 30 *years old.*

TRINIDAD, *widow, sister of Don Pablo,* 35 *years old.*

DANIEL MONTOYA, *in love with Mariana,* 30 *years old.*

DON PABLO, *general,* 48 *years old.*

DON JOAQUIN, *a former protector of Mariana, from* 65 *to* 70 *years old (noble character).*

DON CASTULO, *a rather grotesque archæologist and antiquary,* 56 *years old.*

LUCIANO, *in love with Clara,* 22 *years old.*

Servants, *etc.*

[*Rights of adaptation and stage representation reserved.*]

ACT I.

The scene represents a drawing-room adorned with elegance. Doors at the sides and in the back centre. Night. All splendidly lit up. A little "At Home" is taking place. CLARA *is discovered seated:* TRINIDAD *enters to her.*

TRIN. I am coming to keep you company, Clarita.

CLARA. Are you tired of hearing music?

TRIN. (*sitting down beside* CLARA). I only like music when I am in the Teatro Real. There, it costs me very dear, so it should be very good. The only things worth considering are those that cost money.

CLARA. True enough : that's why men are most fond of the women for whom they make most sacrifices.

TRIN. That's why Daniel is so fond of the enchanting Mariana.

CLARA. And that's why your brother, Don Pablo, our heroic general, is so fond of the divine Mariana.

TRIN. How am I to know?

CLARA. Don't deny it.

TRIN. No, darling, I'll not deny it. Although I think my heroic brother has plunged into a war in which there will be more defeats than victories.

CLARA. One victory, that of the wedding, will be enough for him ; and afterwards—taking into consideration Mariana's character—there are no disasters to be feared. Moreover, Don Pablo, like a true soldier, would take bloody vengeance for any such.

TRIN. The wedding is very doubtful.

CLARA. Why? Common sense counsels it. Mariana is a widow who is hardly a widow, and is almost a child : beautiful as a mid-day sun ; rich with an incalculable richness—for half America is hers ; a reputation without blemish ; a virtue flawless as marble.

TRIN. Perhaps the reason of her being so virtuous is that she bears such a resemblance to marble. The Venus of Milo would resist all the amorous assaults of all the wearers of dress-coats or smoking jackets without an evil thought passing through her most beautiful head, without a single tremor agitating her heart of stone.

CLARA. But, after all, she is virtuous. And as for your brother . . . ah ! your brother is a soldier of lofty exploits and pure fame ; loyal, energetic, attractive ; with his forty-eight years he is worth many men of thirty ; and in the political world he will mount very high.

TRIN. We are agreed that Pablo is heroic and sympathetic, and that Mariana is rich, very beautiful, and virtuous ?

CLARA. Quite so.

TRIN. Well, mark me : our dear Mariana must be very virtuous, no doubt, but she flirts horribly with Daniel.

CLARA (laughing). You call that flirtation ? Say that she roasts him at a slow fire, that she torments him without pity, that she plays with him as a cat with a mouse : strokes him, sticks her claws in him ; lets him go, springs on to him : makes fond grimaces at him, and covers him with blood. This is not coquetry; it is more like hatred, cruelty. Poor Daniel! if he does not fly, he will either be driven mad, or will blow his brains out.

TRIN. Climaxes like those are only found in melodrama. He will either be undeceived and marry some one else . . . or he will get wedded to Mariana.

CLARA. But I tell you she hates him. Am I not likely to know her? When she looks at him she fixes her eyes as when she used to quarrel with a girl at college, and fly at her, and bite and scratch her. Believe me, if the usages of society allowed it, she would bite and scratch Daniel.

TRIN. Ah! Clarita, how dangerous that is!

CLARA. For Daniel.

TRIN. No, dear, for Mariana. Listen—I will tell you in confidence. The first thing that I felt with regard to my poor, dear Paco—may he rest in peace! —was an invincible desire to bite his hands—because they were always beautifully white and well cared for . . . you understand? (*Wipes her eyes.*)

CLARA (*laughing*). What you tell me is remarkable. Before I was married I never had any desire to bite my dear Castulo. Since our marriage—I've many times longed to do so.

TRIN. But if Mariana hates Daniel, as you say, why does she receive him in her house? why does she call him to her and attract his attention?

CLARA. I don't know. It must be because she delights in tormenting him. Mariana is very good, but she is . . . how shall I say it? . . . somewhat cruel.

TRIN. Certainly. Mariana is very good; but at heart . . . at heart . . . (*mysteriously*) God knows what Mariana is,

CLARA. Do you know what she is?—Selfish.

TRIN. I know her to be very cold-natured.

CLARA. No; she is dried up at the heart.

TRIN. She likes nobody.

CLARA. Because she has no feeling.   There it is—
she has no feeling.

TRIN. And she does not believe in anybody or in
anything.

CLARA. But, in spite of all, she is very good.

Enter DON JOAQUIN.

TRIN. She is indeed ; and I am very fond of her.

CLARA. And she is so lovely !

TRIN. Most lovely !

CLARA. Don Joaquin.

JOAQ. You are now speaking kindly of some friend.

TRIN. That's true.

JOAQ. Was I not sure of it?   It may be known
from your faces. . . . You wore the faces of the
"grand panegyrists," as Don Castulo would say.

CLARA. That is so.   We were speaking

JOAQ. Of the mistress of the house?

TRIN. Quite so—of Mariana.

JOAQ. And you did not require much inspiration
to

CLARA. To what?

JOAQ. To end by deifying her?   (*apart*) by
drawing and quartering her.

CLARA. Not very much.

JOAQ. Then I shall assist you.   Let us continue our
raising of Mariana to the rank of the divinities.

TRIN. You love her greatly.

CLARA. You were always very fond of her.

TRIN. You have been almost like a father to her.

JOAQ. Not quite so.   But, indeed, I take a true

interest in her. And at my age a man may interest himself, as I do, in a young woman like Mariana without fear of your deifying us. So say I—if you will take my opinion . . . though I am not very much to be relied upon.

CLARA (*laughing*). No, señor, you're not indeed.

TRIN. (*laughing*). No, señor; you are still dangerous.

CLARA. Dangerous when you have the opportunity.

JOAQ. What's that you are telling me? You really flatter me. I must beg Don Pablo's permission to pay my court to you, Trinidad. I shall ask a licence from Don Castulo, our prince of archæologists, to deliver to you, Clarita, a course of practical lessons in archæology.

CLARA. Put away your flowers of rhetoric, and let us return to Mariana.

JOAQ. Then we had not made an end of her?

CLARA. No, señor; a great deal still remained to be said about the enchanting young widow.

TRIN. A widow! But she can scarcely be called one. She goes to be married, or her father proceeds to have her married, by power of attorney, to an immensely rich American: he ships her off by the first steamer; the divine betrothed disembarks—to meet the dead body of her bridegroom. Tell me conscientiously: is that being a widow? (*To* DON JOAQUIN.)

JOAQ. Well, let us call her "a widow by power of attorney." You are not one of that fashion, Trinidad?

TRIN. No, señor. Poor Paco!

JOAQ. And you—you are not a widow in that way, Clarita?

CLARA. Not in any way. Have you forgotten Castulo?

JOAQ. True! true! What a head I have! . . .
Castulo!   the high priest of archæology!
Humph, here he comes at the conjuration.

CLARA. And he comes with Luciano; poor lad!

JOAQ. What supplicating looks that poor lad directs
toward you, Clarita—to save him!

CLARA. Leave them alone; Castulo is initiating
him into the mysteries of archæology.

JOAQ. Throw him a life-buoy.

CLARA. Exactly. And Castulo will bear up behind.
(*The three talk in whispers and laugh.*)

Enter DON CASTULO *and* LUCIANO. CLARA, TRINI-
DAD, *and* DON JOAQUIN *form a group to
the left of the spectator.* DON CASTULO *and*
LUCIANO *come slowly from the other drawing-
rooms and take their places also to leftward.*
DON CASTULO *is explaining with enthusiasm.*
LUCIANO *listens courteously, but does not cease
to direct glances towards* CLARA.

CAST. Undeceive yourself, Luciano; there is nothing
more curious, more instructive, and, I would almost
dare to say, more profound, than the history of that
utensil so prosaic in appearance. Oh! the history of
the comb from the remotest times—from the cavern
of the primeval bear, and the prehistoric hyæna, and
the bristly elephant down to our days—is the history
of humanity! Do you doubt it?

LUC. I do not doubt it, Don Castulo. But there I
see your good lady. . . .

CAST. (*detaining him*). Don't believe me on my
word alone. We archæologists are inclined to be
vain; but I have a collection of combs!
Ah! . . .

LUC. I think Clarita is calling me.

CAST. (*looking aside for a moment*). No, she is not calling you. You shall call on us to-morrow and pass a pleasant time with us.

LUC. I? With whom?

CAST. Yes, you—with that unrivalled collection.

LUC. Pah!—the collection of combs?

CAST. The British Museum offered me four thousand pounds sterling for it.

LUC. And you did not sell it?

CAST. Sell it! I! I said to myself, "Now I may call you genuine combs!" I have—on my word of honour—I have combs made of the backbone of a fish, of porcupine's quills, of wood, of cane, of bone, of crystal, of various metals, even of horn.

LUC. Horn!

CAST. And of bull's horn, indeed. Not to be denied, señor—not to be denied. Always remember this maxim : where there is a graft there are various grafts; and where there are various grafts or thorns there is a comb.

LUC. The devil! Can it be true? I think . I now really think . . . (*Wishing to go to* CLARA ; DON CASTULO *detains him.*)

CAST. You must breakfast with us to-morrow, and you shall see wonders. I have combs of all shapes and of all ages : rectilineal, curvilineal, triangular, polygonal, representative, non-representative, smooth, carven, Doric, Ionic, Corinthian, and composite. I have them from Egypt, Assyria, Greece . . . there have you grafts, indeed ! . . . from Rome . . . there have you combs ! I have those which were shattered by barbarians—a sort of petrifactive devastation—for those people preferred the thistle to the comb for the smoothing of their hair. I have even a comb which is said to have belonged to

Charlemagne! 1 have actually . actually another
comb which is declared to have been used by La
Cava!¹ . . . Pure legends! For on the point of
combs one must walk with great care.

LUC. Yes, Clarita, I am coming. (CLARA *has not
called him.*) Excuse me, Don Castulo; your wife is
decidedly calling me. (DON CASTULO, *growing still
more enthusiastic in his discourse, is not in time to
detain him, and* LUCIANO *approaches* CLARA.)

CAST. (*aside*). How impertinent these women are!
Poor Luciano was enchanted. And you   (*Approaching the group.*)

TRIN. (*to* DON CASTULO). Did you say anything?

CAST. Nothing. You come away from those others.
(*Taking her apart.*)

TRIN. Were you tired of playing billiards?

CAST. I never play. It is an empty game. To
aim a stroke at a ball, in order that a ball may roll
Do you think, my friend, that that noble substance,
ivory—pure, classical, with all the softness and deli-
cacy characteristic of the touch of feminine things,
and all the sudden energy of masculine strength—do
you think, I repeat, that ivory was created to be
transformed into diminutive balls, and to endure
blows from the cues of four idlers? Ah! if the
elephants knew it, how they would raise the sky with
their trumpetings! Make out of ivory artistic little
figures ; make combs—let me put a case in point—
which may sink voluptuously into the tresses of a
beautiful woman—everything, except billiard-balls.
And, positively, I have in my collection .

TRIN. Excuse me ; I must find my brother. . . .

---

¹ Florinda La Cava, the lover of Rodrigo, the last of the
Gothic kings.

CAST. We shall look for him together. (*Preparing to accompany her.*)

TRIN. Many thanks. Don Joaquin wants you.— Don Joaquin. (*Calling.*)

CAST. Wants me? . . . Don Joaquin. . . . (*Going towards him.*)

JOAQ. (*meeting* CASTULO). Did you call me?

CAST. I did not call you . . . but it's all the same ; we'll suppose that I did call you. (*Taking possession of* DON JOAQUIN.)

TRIN. (*she will have approached* CLARA *and* LUCIANO *while uttering the previous sentences, and now says to them*). So, good-bye for the present.

CLARA. Are you going already?

TRIN. No; I shall come back .... when the danger is over (*pointing to* DON CASTULO).

(CLARA *and* LUCIANO *to the right, speaking in whispers;* DON CASTULO *and* DON JOAQUIN *to the left.*)

CAST. What high-strung nerves women have! They cannot be at ease for five minutes : cannot fix their attention for two minutes : cannot listen for half a minute.

JOAQ. Cannot listen. That's not always the case. (*Turning a glance towards* CLARA, *who listens with interest, while* LUCIANO *speaks with much emphasis.*)

CAST. Then it must be when you speak to them of fashions. But speak to them of serious things : of my collections, for example. . . .

JOAQ. (*appalled*). Yes. I already know . . . about those collections !

CAST. Very well. I was speaking of them to Trinidad. Now you would have listened for an hour consecutively. . . .

JOAQ. I hardly think so.

CAST. Why, you heard me yesterday for three hours ; and you heard me breathlessly. Well, Trinidad would not listen to me even during the most insignificant space of time.

JOAQ. What do you say? . . . She would not ! . . . She would not listen to you? Impossible ! . . . Do you hear? . . . Do you hear? (*Approaching, with great demonstrations of horror,* CLARA *and* LUCIANO, *in order to take part in their conversation and escape from* DON CASTULO.)

CLARA. What do you say, Don Joaquin?

JOAQ. That Trinidad finds no amusement in Archæology ! Repeat that, Don Castulo.

LUCIANO. Is it possible?

CAST. It is possible. Ah ! (*to* LUCIANO.) People are not all like you. And, by the way (*turning to* CLARA), I have requested Luciano to breakfast with us to-morrow. I have to show him two or three acquisitions. I have fallen in with a Genoese majolica, which will send you raving.

LUC. I can believe it. Clarita, your house contains treasures.

CAST. You may well say that to me.

LUC. How I envy you, Don Castulo !

CAST. (*laughing*). So I imagine. But they are all my own. And I have added Amenhotep I., Amenhotep II., and Amenhotep III. to the Egyptian gallery. You did not know that.

LUC. (*to* CLARA). Don't you remember that Trinidad is waiting for you ?

CLARA (*rising*). It's true. (*To her husband.*) She expects us for the customary game of ombre.

LUC. Excuse us, Don Castulo. (*To* CLARA.) Shall we go there ?

CLARA. Let us go.

CAST. But does she positively expect you?

CLARA. Positively.

[*Exeunt* CLARA *and* LUCIANO.

JOAQ. She expects me also. [*Going out.*

CAST. (*taking him by the arm*). No; not you. There are four already. Pablo, Trinidad, Clarita, and Luciano. You would make one too many.

JOAQ. I am one too many everywhere.

CAST. You are never one too many for me.—I was saying that my Egyptian collection is simply marvellous. I have some twenty hybrid little figures . . . thus we called them. . . . When Luciano saw them, I thought he would turn faint. I have the Man of Straw, the Winged Horse; I have the Human Ox and egad! the last-named strongly resembles yourself.

JOAQ. Many thanks.

CAST. Give those thanks to the Pharaonic artist. And, passing on to Assyria, what would you say if you saw my collection of beards of Adrammelech and of Sarasar the parricide? And then the collection of eyebrow tweezers of the wife of Assurbanipal! With them I am now and then seized with the humour of plucking out the superfluous hairs on the eyebrows of Clarita.

JOAQ. But those are the refinements of Archæology.

CAST. And pleasures of which you have no idea. (*Becoming animated.*) Time becomes contracted, races commingle, the ages are confounded together. I live amongst all the men who have been, I jostle against them; we are almost as familiar with each other as bosom friends. "Give me the tweezers,

Assurbanipal, my wife is waiting." Or else, " Nabo-
palasar, give me the brush, I have a mud-stain on my
trousers." With this pocket-handkerchief Phidias
wiped his forehead ; in these little shoes perspired the
tiny feet of a Moorish queen. Oh ! grandeurs of
history ; oh ! littlenesses of private life, I have you
both in my house in the rigorous order of classifica-
tion. The immense wheel of the epic runs in a
groove with the insignificant pinion of the domestic.
What more? In one glass case I have a comb with a
quantity of hairs, which may have been from the
beard of Assurbanipal. Assurbanipal, Don Joaquin !
In these times, as they vulgarly say, and pardon me
the phrase, now that we are in confidence,—in the
present day we " laugh in the beard " of some one ;
but to " laugh in the beard " of Assurbanipal on his
throne of Nineveh, at a distance of thirty centuries—
can you understand anything more magnificent ?

JOAQ. Yes, sir. (*Aside.*) To do the same to me in
this historic moment.

CAST. You are right. There is something more
magnificent. For I may tell you . . .

JOAQ. At present it is not possible. . . .

CAST. Why ?

JOAQ. Because Mariana and Daniel are coming
here.

CAST. And what then ?

JOAQ. Then they must be left alone to prepare the
Archæology of the future.

CAST. True.

JOAQ. So good-bye for the present.

CAST. I am going with you. The company of so
enlightened a man cannot be sufficiently appreciated
by me.

JOAQ. (*in a tone of despair*). Nabucodonosor !

CAST. I have also something about me of Nabu-codonosor.

JOAQ. Something! No; a great deal. [*Exeunt.*

Enter MARIANA *and* DANIEL, *by the right.*

MAR. (*bursts into a laugh, and follows with her eyes* DON CASTULO *and* DON JOAQUIN). It's delightful, most delightful. Ha, ha, ha!

DAN. How merry you have become all at once, Mariana! What are you laughing at? . . . Pardon me; but that laughter.

MAR. Set your mind at ease, Daniel. I am not laughing at you. I am laughing at those two—especially at Don Joaquin.

DAN. At Don Joaquin!

MAR. At my good friend; at my respectable guardian; at my dear Don Joaquin.

DAN. Why?

MAR. Don't you see Don Castulo bearing him off? (*Laughing.*) Under the power of Don Castulo, who will explain to him. . . . how do I know what he'll explain to him!—Don Joaquin will now be driven mad.

DAN. And you delight in the misery of that good gentleman who loves you so much!

MAR. I don't delight in his misery: I laugh at it—two very distinct things.

DAN. If you treat your friends thus, how do you treat your enemies?

MAR. In the same way. I find no great difference between the one and the other of them. Friend enemy . . . all depends, as Don Castulo would say, on the historic moment when you consider him. You are my friend to-day; to-morrow you will be my enemy.

DAN. Never!

MAR. *Never* is the most useless word in the dictionary. For goodness' sake, Daniel, don't come to me this evening with romanticisms which are out of fashion now ; and permit me to laugh without malice at my dearest Don Joaquin, who is being marched triumphantly through my drawing-rooms by Don Castulo, as a conqueror of ancient times might have dragged behind his chariot of war a vanquished king.

DAN. Ah! Mariana, Don Castulo is not the only one who drags through your drawing-rooms the poor slaves enchained to a triumphal car.

MAR. There is another who is guilty of similar inhumanities?

DAN. I think so.

MAR. And that other despot is myself?

DAN. Yourself: and you know it.

MAR. Good: then I will not be inhuman, nor despotic, nor cruel, nor carry slaves about with me. I break the chain and give them liberty. (*Rising as if to go away.*)

DAN. No, for God's love, Mariana ; don't go away. The chain cannot be broken. And even if you should break it, the slave would follow you to the end of the world, to the end of life.

MAR. These fits of exaggeration make me nervous, and, furthermore, they make you and me look ridiculous.

DAN. Do you want us to speak seriously?

MAR. Speak seriously! That would be a cruelty. But, in short, speak—and as you please. (*Sits down.*)

DAN. Mariana, do you love me or hate me? I don't know : tell me the truth yourself.

MAR. (*laughs*). That he may love me if I love him, that he may hate me if I hate him.

DAN. That I may live . . . or that I may die; but always for my Mariana.

MAR. What bursts of profound passion !

DAN. Don't sneer at me.

MAR. I am not sneering.

DAN. Then answer me fairly : is it hatred, is it love ?

MAR. (*approaching him and looking at him with something of coquetry, something of tenderness*). Well . . . I don't know, myself. (*A pause; they look at each other for some moments.*)

DAN. Perhaps you say what you feel.

MAR. I am very frank.

DAN. But why did you speak of hating me ? (*In a softened tone.*) I adore Mariana as one adores the angels. I think of you night and day with infinite fondness; if by any chance you call me, saying simply: "Daniel!" all the fibres of my being tremble, as a man might tremble who is summoned by his God. Is that a motive for hatred? What reason have you to abhor me ?

MAR. (*listening to him with a kind of pleasure*). None; and that makes it all the more agreeable. A hatred with a motive is a melodramatic hatred; a hatred without cause is a most artistic, most refined hatred, worthy of you and worthy of me, who are people of good taste.

DAN. So that you hate me ?

MAR. If you are tiresome, what must I do ?

DAN. Mariana, Mariana, why do you delight in torturing me ?

MAR. How am I to know? Come, let's see: let us discuss the subject together. Let's begin: let's treat it archæologically; let's recall the time when I did not know you.

DAN. And when I did not know you, either.

MAR. Chance caused us to see each other for the first time.

DAN. Chance it was. I was passing one day through the street, my father leaning on my arm— for the poor man was, and is, very ill. . . .

MAR. Does he suffer much?

DAN. Very much, Mariana.

MAR. Poor señor! Some day we must take out the carriage and go and see him. His country house is two or three leagues from Madrid, is it not?

DAN: At most; and how grateful to you the poor old man would be!

MAR. Go on. You were passing by with your father, who was so enveloped in rugs that I could not see him. You I did see. (*Laughing.*)

DAN. And I you. It was the first time I had seen you.

MAR. The first . . . and when will the last be? Who can pierce into the future! (*Pensively.*)

DAN. Do you want it to be soon?

MAR. No: frankly; I do not want it. (*Softly.*) How sad it would be not to see you!

DAN. Mariana!

MAR. How dull and how wearisome existence would be without a person to . . .

DAN. To *love?*

MAR. What impudence! I said no such thing.

DAN. Then . . . to torment.

MAR. Torment or love, it's all the same.

DAN. Then let it be; I accept the torment and the affection.

MAR. For the present—let the former suffice.

DAN. How cruel you are!

MAR. Get on, get on with the romantic first meeting. You passing with your father, and I in an open carriage waiting at the door of a shop. Isn't that it?

DAN. And I looking at you, and thinking, "How happy I should be if that woman would address a word to me, a single word! Just to hear her voice!"

MAR. Well, since that time you must have been very happy, for we have spoken a great deal together.

DAN. I have been so.

MAR. And nothing else happened? Because I don't remember.

DAN. Yes; a poor child, ragged, almost naked, with hungry face, asked an alms from you.

MAR. It's true. These abandoned children! (*Sadly and pensively.*)

DAN. You looked at her with pity, with sympathy, with affection, and your beautiful eyes were bedimmed with a rain-cloud of tears. You gave her a piece of money, and told her your private address, which I heard plainly. And I thought, "She is very good."

MAR. The proof was conclusive. (*Mockingly.*)

DAN. You raised your glance, you fixed it on me, and your face had changed. Your first look had been like a sunbeam which falls upon a drop of rain and is transformed into a rainbow. Your second look was like the same sunbeam when it wanders on and falls upon a dark and lonely cloud, and is converted into a purple reflex of it. And I reluctantly thought, "That's a very bad woman."

MAR. The case is clear: you had been guilty of an impertinence and I could not restrain my annoyance. You called to the child and gave her an alms, as if to say, "I must do likewise; between us two we shall succour this poor creature; now, madame, there's a tie that binds us." That's what you thought, and I thought · "How impertinent that interesting young fellow is!"

DAN. Mariana! . . .

MAR. Yes, you may complain, and I have involuntarily called you interesting; I had almost said prepossessing.

DAN. I shall be what you please; let me conclude. I made inquiries and found that you were the daughter of a rich banker who had died in America. I sought for some one to introduce̅ me to your house .

MAR. And I received you very well, did I not?

DAN. Certainly.

MAR. And since then, for all that you may say, I have not treated you badly. I allow you to speak to me of your affection, to accompany me everywhere. Come, I have almost compromised my reputation for you.

DAN. No, not that, Mariana. To beg you on my knees—if that be necessary—that you should be my wife, is not to compromise you.

MAR. Your wife! . . . (laughing.) What an idea!

DAN. Why not? You are rich . . . it is true . . .

MAR. Who is thinking of that?

DAN. But so am I, though not so rich; you are young and beautiful. . . .

MAR. (jestingly). You are not old, and I have already said what I'll not now repeat. . . .

DAN. Is your position high? My father's has been so. Are you anxious to mount higher? I shall mount for you. I deliver myself up to you entirely, unconditionally. My life, my happiness, my soul, my honour, all the conceptions of my brain, all the pulsations of my heart, even to the last drop of my

blood, everything is yours. To you I shall be as a
brother, as a father, as a slave, as a lover ; all ! Say
to me, " Be my adorer," and, to adore you the sooner,
I shall bow down with such violence as to shatter my
forehead against the stones! Say to me, "Fool,
amuse me," and I shall adorn my skull with cap and
bells. Say to me, " That creature vexes me," then I
shall kill the creature and become a murderer. Say
to me, " Love me," and on that day, if you have not
a heart, I shall die in your arms ; if you have a heart,
you shall die in mine !

MAR. Not so fast ; not so fast, Daniel, we are not
playing a scene in a comedy. Still, do you know
that if all this is true you must be very fond of me.
(*Looking closely at him with curiosity, interest, and
sympathy.*) But don't you think that such things
have been often said in this world and that they have
nearly always been lies ? (*Growing dubious.*)

DAN. Not on my lips, Mariana.

MAR. Well, look you, whether falsehood or truth,
you have said all that with such fire, with an accent
of such profound emotion, that I believe it—provisionally. Don't interrupt me. This evening I want us
both to be in good humour, both to be happy ; happy
—provisionally. To-morrow, God will tell.
(*Stopping another movement on the part of* DANIEL.)
Don't interrupt me. What you have said to me has
gone to my very soul ; after all I am a woman, and
women are deceived so easily. I also feel longings
to love. Do you think not ? I also am pleased with
the affection in which I ¡may be held. And to be
much loved ought to be a very great happiness—is it
not true? To think that a man, good, generous,
brave, intellectual, is dying for one ! " I can make
him laugh, I can make him cry ! " That's delightful.

To hold the heart of a being so strong and so deserving as you, between one's hands, as one might say—between these hands—so very small, so feeble ; and I squeeze and press his heart to suffocation, and I fondle it and it palpitates to very madness. And nobody in the world can do as much for that man's happiness as I ! Believe me, Daniel, that makes one proud. On witnessing in you so much love, so much self-denial, such abandonment of your own existence to the will of such a poor woman as myself, I feel impulses to repay your fondness with a fondness quite as great . . . no—greater ! No one shall outvie me, when I set myself to be generous. Go on as you have begun, go on—and some day I shall not be able to contain myself, and I will say to you like a mad-woman, " Daniel, Daniel, I love you with all my soul." (*In this speech there is evident sincerity; she secretly feels what she says, although she endeavours at times to assume a tone of jocularity, especially at the beginning.*)

DAN. But do you feel all that you have said ? My God, I don't believe it. Can it be true ? (*With a movement of impetuous joy.*)

MAR. (*resuming her airs of coquetry, ana arresting his enthusiasm*). A *provisional* truth : a *hypothetical* truth : for this night—while these emotions last. When they pass off, I know neither what I shall think nor what I shall say.

DAN. You will end by driving me mad.

MAR. God help me, nothing satisfies you. I who was so full of joy ! I felt as I have not felt for a long time. I imagined myself a restless child. . I even had my projects . . . ravings ! . . . But with my projects and my ravings *I associated you.* (*With an alluring and almost tender accent.*)

DAN. Is it true? Ah, Mariana! Let those ravings come and let us both plunge into them.

MAR. No! not now; you have made me sad. (*She feigns an endearing sadness.*)

DAN. Pardon me; forget my impertinences. Let me see, let me see . . . tell me what were the projects.

MAR. (*mysteriously*). They were projects for this evening.

DAN. I don't understand.

MAR. Night is the great concealer of madcap escapades. The light of the sun is like a prying iudge; the shadows of the night are wayward. And I . . . Shall I say it? .

DAN. Yes, Mariana.

MAR. This night there takes place in the Real a grand masked ball; a charity ball. And I was thinking of a hood, a mask—and the arm of Daniel to take me to my box.

DAN. We two.

MAR. (*correcting the impertinence of* DANIEL, *but without seeming to have understood it*). With Clarita and Trinidad. I spoke to them and very likely everything is arranged.

DAN. (*with a kind of suspicion*). And who else?

MAR. Luciano, who will give his arm to Clarita. Don Castulo (*laughing*) in all solemnity escorting Trinidad. And with me . . . I have already mentioned my escort; that is to say, if you are deserving.

DAN. Nobody else?

MAR. We count on no one else.

DAN. So that Don Pablo? . . .

MAR. I was not thinking of Don Pablo   unless you despise my company.

DAN. How cruel you are! . . . No, how good! . . . An angel! . . . Such an appearance do angels wear.

MAR. (*laughing*). Do angels go to the ball at the Real wearing hoods and masks? I wasn't aware of that.

DAN. Yes, señora—and on the arm of Daniel.

MAR. What madcaps they must be!

DAN. Well, let us go there; it is very late, Mariana; it is very late.

MAR. There's plenty of time. And we have to arrange several things. For instance, my attendant knight must have a device. Will this flower be a good device? (*Taking out one which she wears in her bosom.*)

DAN. With this flower. . . . (*Taking it with frantic eagerness and trying to fix it in his coat, but not succeeding.*)

MAR. Yes; I know already. With that flower you will scale the heavens or descend to the bottomless abyss! All such enterprises you are capable of accomplishing. What you can't do is to fix that flower into your buttonhole—unless I help you.

DAN. And would you do it? . . .

MAR. Help my knight? . . . Why not? . . . It is the obligation of the dame, and it is a work of mercy. (*Fixing the flower.*)

DAN. Of mercy, Mariana!

MAR. I think it is more a mercy. . . .

DAN. It is not yet . . . it has not remained fixed (*That she may not go away from him.*) It is going to fall.

MAR. Yes . . . Yes . . . It has kept fast. And now have sense, for here comes Don Pablo.

Enter DON PABLO.

DAN. The devil take Don Pablo! What business have these military men in drawing-rooms? To the field, to the field of honour, to die with glory ! That's what they are for, and not to come between Mariana and myself.

PABLO (*to* MARIANA). Do you permit me to approach ?

MAR. I permit it and I request it. And I beg you to take a seat here, at my side. (*They both sit down.* DANIEL *remains on foot.*)

PABLO. But is my conversation agreeable to you ?

MAR. Good Heavens, general ! You know it is.

PABLO. I am no speaker of gallantries.

MAR. True affection is not on the lips.

PABLO. It is in the heart.

DAN. When the affection is not very great it remains there. When it is abundant it overflows from the lips.

MAR. According to the fitness of things, Daniel ; it depends on the capacity of the vessel ; when it is small it quickly overflows.

PABLO. Well said.

MAR. Well said . . . but it is well said because it has been in defence of you. (*To* DON PABLO.)

PABLO. Thanks, Mariana.

DAN. It is not a very brilliant part—that of a soldier who requires to be defended.

PABLO. Here I need and I accept the defence of Mariana ; away from here, I alone defend myself as best I can.

MAR. Very well said.

DAN. Then I say . . . (*Impetuously.*)

MAR. You say nothing. You surrender yourself as vanquished. For you have been so, and on your own ground.

PABLO. If you declare me the conqueror, what greater glory could I have '

DAN. If you declare me vanquished, what greater defeat could I suffer!

MAR. But every victory requires a trophy. (*Seeking on her breast for the flower which she had given to* DANIEL.) Ah! . . . I thought I was wearing a flower

DAN. This is the one, Mariana.

MAR. It's true: I did not remember. I'll get one for the general. (*Approaches a branch and plucks a flower.*) Take this, general.

PABLO. Mariana! (*Tries to fix the flower, but goes awkwardly about it.*)

DAN. (*aside*). Ah! . . . she doesn't go near him . she doesn't fix his flower for him.

MAR. Can't you fix it, general?

PABLO. I am very clumsy.

DAN. (*without knowing what he says, and to prevent* MARIANA *from helping* DON PABLO, *approaches the last named with much solicitude*). If you cannot I shall help you.

PABLO. (*looking at him from head to foot*). Thanks: I can do it myself.

MAR. (*laughing*). What a joke! . . . (*aside to* DANIEL.) There's nobody can make himself so ridiculous as a lover.

DAN. (*aside to* MARIANA). Rather than have you go near him to fix that flower, I'd have buried a sword or a bullet in his heart.

MAR. (*aside*). High tragedy!

PABLO. It's done now.

DAN. (*mockingly*). A new victory for the general: it cost labour; but he has conquered, and this time without the help of Mariana.

PABLO. The finest and most enjoyable victories are those which cost much.

DAN. If they don't cost life.

PABLO. They generally do cost life—to the defeated.

DAN. Not always. Just now I was defeated—according to Mariana—and I am full of life.

PABLO. Skirmishes are not always sanguinary.

MAR. You, general, neither can nor ought to risk your noble existence in light skirmishes, but on fields of battle. And now the skirmish has ended. (DON PABLO *and* DANIEL *bow respectfully and preserve silence.*) Will you give me your arm—(*to the General*)—and take me to Trinidad, for I want to speak to her.

PABLO. Señora . . .

DAN. And I, am I to wait?

MAR. As you please, Daniel.

DAN. You said . . .

MAR. Ah! . . . yes . . . it's true. . . . What a head I have to-night! Yes, wait for me, Daniel. I shall come back soon. We have a project, general, of which you are ignorant.

DAN. (*in a supplicating tone*). It is a secret Mariana ! . . .

PABLO. A secret !

MAR. But we shall shortly reveal it to you.

DAN. By God ! . . .

MAR. We shall reveal it to you to-morrow.

[*Exeunt* PABLO *and* MARIANA.

Enter DON JOAQUIN *as if in flight, and turning his head to see if he is pursued by* DON CASTULO.

DAN. That woman will drive me mad.

JOAQ. You say that *that woman* will drive you mad?

DAN. Yes.

JOAQ. Well, *that man* has driven me mad.

DAN. Who?

JOAQ. Don Castulo. I carry within here (*pressing his head*) all the Egyptians, all the Babylonians,— a Babylonian chaos,[1] indeed! All the Greeks, all the Romans, and all the barbarians—the barbarians above all. I carry all the Pharaonic mummies, and all the Merovingian skeletons. I carry . . . Ah! I carry this letter, which seems very urgent. (*Showing a letter which he bears in his hand.*)

DAN. A letter?

JOAQ. For you. It comes from your house, from which it was brought this very moment. A servant of your father brought it.

DAN. From my father! (*Taking the letter hurriedly.*)

JOAQ. He arrived a quarter of an hour since in a carriage, with orders to seek you all over Madrid without losing an instant, and to drive you out to the villa.

DAN. (*reading*). God help me! . . .

JOAQ. What's the matter? Has your father been taken ill?

DAN. It's what I feared. Another fit is expected; my sister is very much alarmed; I must go at once.

JOAQ. Don't be prematurely alarmed. Either the fit will not come on, or he will get over this as he did over the previous one.

DAN. Who knows! . . . In any case, I must go without losing an instant. My poor father! . . .

JOAQ. Then come . . . I shall accompany you as far as the carriage.

DAN. Yes, let us go . . . (*Stopping.*) But I must

---

[1] Babilonia = a perfect Babel.

first take leave of Mariana.   Of Mariana. . . .
Oh ! accursed coincidence !

Re-enter MARIANA *by a side door with a domino or
hood, and a mask in her hand; she enters looking
very merry and affectionate.*

MAR. Here you see me, Daniel. I have not
forgotten our solemn promise! Trinidad, Clarita,
Don Castulo and Luciano will be there. But you are
not coming (*to* DON JOAQUIN) nor Don Pablo. You
steady going people must remain to play at ombre.

DAN. Mariana !

MAR. What a gloomy expression on your face!
Are you vexed ? Don Joaquin, Daniel is vexed, and
I know why. He considers that I have been ex-
cessively amiable to Don Pablo. Poor Daniel !

DAN. Mariana.

JOAQ. (*aside—walking to the back*). The three
hundred and sixty-fifth reconciliation they have had
within the past year !

MAR. (*looks at him for a few moments, then approaches him and says in a somewhat tremulous voice*).
Don't be jealous : if the day should come for me to
fall in love . . . I'll not be answerable for the coming
of that day—eh ? but if it should come, it will only be
with one man : only with one man—whom I know.

DAN. (*eagerly*). With whom ?

MAR. (*a pause : they gaze at each other*). Come to
the Real, and I'll tell you in the private box.

DAN. (*desperately*). I cannot.

MAR. (*in displeasure*). I don't understand.

DAN. I have just received this letter . . . my
father is ill. . . . I must set out this very moment for
his country seat. I kept back so as to take leave of
you. Forgive me, Mariana,

MAR. I am very sorry. . . . It is natural: you cannot accompany me.

DAN. Perhaps death is waiting for me. . . . And I carry away death in my soul !

MAR. No, Daniel : the first is first. And your father is very ill !

DAN. They write to me in fear lest the fit should come on again.

MAR. But are these, after all, no more than fears? . . . Come, it is not so bad.

DAN. Nothing more than fears . . . but you understand. . . .

MAR. I should think so. Yes, it is very proper. It is very natural that you should be alarmed . . . and that you should go away leaving everything behind me and the whole world.

DAN. Leave you ! . . . Don't say that.   It is that chance pursues me with the most cruel and cunning determination. Leave Mariana !

MAR. There, enough: say no more : go, go, Daniel, and let there be nothing further said about it.

DAN. Mariana

MAR. Parents are sacred. What would I not have given for my mother ? What would I not sacrifice to her memory ? Happiness, pleasure, love . . life ! And you hesitate, Daniel? (*With profound emotion.*) Run quickly to your father, or I shall believe that you are like all men—selfish ! (*The last sentence drily, almost contemptuously. A pause: then, after looking at* DANIEL.) Don Joaquin, will you tell Don Pablo what has happened . . . and see if he will be kind enough to prepare to be my escort?

DAN. Mariana !

JOAQ. With great pleasure.   [*Exit.*

MAR. (*arranging her costume with indifference, and looking in the mirror*). Well, are you not going?

DAN. Mariana . . . don't go to the Real

MAR. Daniel!

DAN. Pardon me. . . . I know it is presumption on my part.

MAR. I shall not give it that name . . . it's a piece of childishness. You have lost your senses.

DAN. Madness, childishness . . . what you like . . . but I implore you with all my soul. That whim is of such little worth to you. What will it cost you to please me? And I suffer so much . . . I suffer so much. Jealousy! . . . Anger . . . envy . . . envy of that man! . . . I even forget my father. . . Don't go.

MAR. Don't persist. You have no authority to make a slave of me. That which I began by laughing at as childishness I shall conclude by resenting as impertinence.

DAN. Well, don't go with Don Pablo.

MAR. After my having requested him to accompany me! Good God, do you want to make me look ridiculous? These things cannot be done, Daniel. And that I esteem you and have consideration for your annoyance and your state of excitement, is proved by the docility with which I am giving you explanations —which were, indeed, unnecessary. (*Continues to arrange herself.*) Do you fulfil your duties as a son: I shall fulfil other duties . . . duties to society.

DAN. Duties! . . . A caprice! . . . An empty caprice! . . .

MAR. Well, I shall fulfil my caprice. What would you have? I am so selfish and so perverse that I attach more importance to my caprices than to yours.

DAN. For the last time !

MAR. Enough.

Enter CLARA *and* TRINIDAD (*by a side door*) *with dominoes and hoods:* DON CASTULO *and* LUCIANO. *They come in laughing and talking.*

TRIN. (*to* MARIANA). Are you ready?

CLARA. Are we going or not going?

MAR. As soon as Don Pablo arrives. (*The three ladies talk apart.*)

CAST. Well, if I had known ! I have a collection of Venetian masks. .

LUC. I can picture them to myself. . . .

CAST. Perhaps you don't know of the first mask that ever was used?

LUC. I don't know. (*Rushes away:* DON CASTULO *follows him.*)

CAST. Then I shall tell you.

CLARA (*to* DANIEL). So you can't accompany us? What a pity ! . . . Especially for the cause.

TRIN. (*to* DANIEL). But is there matter for anxiety?

DAN. I don't know.

MAR. Let's hope it's a false alarm. But don't be detained on our account. Leave these nonsensical heads to be delivered up to their follies. Here comes Don Pablo.

Enter DON PABLO *and* DON JOAQUIN. MARIANA *goes to meet the former.*

So you will accompany us . . . and accompany me?

PABLO. To be with you where would I not go?

MAR. Always so good ! Always so amiable ! These are what I call sacrifices ! A person like you to take part in our escapades ! Thanks, general, thanks! . . . Good-bye, Daniel, I hope sincerely that you will find your father well. It is possible that on your return here you will not find me, as I think of going for a few days to La Granja . . . Would you like to accompany me there, Don Pablo?

PABLO. I am a soldier, and obedience to superiors is a matter of duty with me. I am a gentleman, and obedience to a lady is a law of gallantry.

MAR. Here's a surrender!—you others take notice. Good-bye, Don Joaquin. Good-bye, Daniel; good wishes . . . till I see you again . . . whenever that may be. (*Giving* DANIEL *her hand.*)

DAN. (*in a hard, low voice*). I don't wish you to go.

MAR. Daniel, for God's sake. . . . March on (*To* DON PABLO.) Your arm. Go on, go on. (*All going to the door.*)

CLARA. To the Real and to supper!

TRIN. To the supper and the champagne.

[*Exeunt* CLARA *and* TRINIDAD.

MAR. *En avant! le drapeau est engagé.* Lead us to victory, my dear general.

PABLO. And where is the victory?

MAR. And does a general ask that? Where some one may be conquered.

[*Exeunt* PABLO *and* MARIANA.

CAST. (*to* LUCIANO). Well, no one shall conquer me in the possession of masks, dominoes, caricature masks, pasteboard masks, and all the masks that ever were invented.

LUC. I believe it. [*Exeunt* CASTULO *and* LUCIANO.

DAN. I cannot do it. . . . I will not leave her . . . Mariana!

JOAQ. You cannot be false to your duty. Go where your obligation as a son calls you!

DAN. But that woman !

JOAQ. She is a woman, and your father is your father.

DAN. A woman who will be my damnation ! Have no fear. Now, to where my father suffers. Afterwards, to where she enjoys herself. Afterwards . . . afterwards . . . how can I know . . . how can I know into what abyss we shall roll together !

JOAQ. Poor Daniel !

DAN. I shall return, Mariana.   [*Exeunt.*

END OF ACT I.

ACT II.

SCENE—*A drawing-room in the mansion of* MARIANA *differing from that of Act I. Adorned with luxury. In the background two doors which look on to the garden.*
TIME—*Day : towards the close of afternoon.*

Enter CLARA, TRINIDAD, *and* LUCIANO.

TRIN. That is to say, we are all bringing to this visit our *objective,* as Pablo says when he speaks of war.

CLARA. All.

LUC. All ! (*Looking at* CLARA.)

CLARA (*to* TRINIDAD). Which is yours, if one may know ?

TRIN. I have already given you an indication of it, and in your case neither my brother nor I could have secrets. I am Minister Plenipotentiary, and I come as representative of the general. (*In a mysterious tone.*)

CLARA. That's understood. To ask in all solemnity the hand of Mariana.

TRIN. Not yet ; these are preliminary negociations. My brother cannot expose himself to a repulse, and previous to the *Official Act*, it is imperative that Mariana should tell me in frankness what is the state

39

of her mind.   She notices Pablo very much ; respects him, admires him, shows exceptional favour towards him—you cannot picture to yourself how amiable she was to my brother during the eight days that they passed at La Granja.   In any other woman it would be equivalent to saying, " Declare your intentions." In Mariana . . . I don't know.

LUC. She also distinguishes Daniel by great marks of favour.

TRIN. Daniel was not at La Granja.

LUC. Because he was attending to Señor de Montoya . . . until the danger should have passed away.   There was danger there of being left without a father ; danger here of being left without a bride. The land of life is sown with the seed of dangers ; and what a harvest springs from that seed time !

TRIN. Daniel is nothing more to Mariana than a toy, a subject of diversion. (*To* LUCIANO.) Undeceive yourself ; if she cared for him she would not martyr him as she does.   At times it arouses pity.

CLARA. But if Mariana be so cruel, if you have such a bad opinion of our good friend, why do you accept her as the wife of Pablo ?

TRIN. No, dear, this is not having a bad opinion of Mariana.   Good Heavens ! must a woman be considered bad because she torments a man ?   Where should we be coming to ?   It is only taking by antici- pation the revenge which the husband will afterwards wreak upon her.   (*Laughing.*)

CLARA (*to* LUCIANO). You hear that, now.

LUC. (*to* TRINIDAD). Many thanks in the name of the sex.

TRIN. Of what sex ?

LUC. Of mine—of the stronger sex.

TRIN. I didn't mean it for you.

CLARA. Poor Luciano! Don't you torment him; my husband tortures him quite enough. (*Laughing.*)

LUC. Ah! . . . Ah! Don Castulo.

TRIN. Besides, if there are men so worthless and so pusillanimous as to let themselves be tortured . . . away with them! Why, Mariana never treats Pablo in this way. And if they eventually marry, Pablo will be the master. Respectful, but energetic; loving, but . not long-suffering; and these coquettish outbreaks . . . will have come to an end.

CLARA. It's true. Don Pablo, in any case, will be the physician of his own honour.

LUC. (*in a low voice to* CLARA). He was so, or was on the point of being so, with his first wife, as the tale runs.

CLARA (*aside*). Silence!

LUC. Well, the general is a great personage and an heroic general; but, for a husband . . . (*aside*) I prefer the Archæologist.

TRIN. Now, dear Clarita, I have confided my secret to you. And you, what brings you to Mariana's mansion to-day? This is not a day on which the lady of the house receives.

CLARA. I also come as an ambassadress.

TRIN. And you? (*To* LUCIANO.)

LUC. I come as an attaché to the embassy.

CLARA. But the business that brings me is not so transcendental as yours. Within a few days Castulo inaugurates his Saloon of Mexican Antiquities, and he wishes to solemnise the ceremony by giving a breakfast to his intimate friends. I am coming personally to invite Mariana; my husband will have already personally invited Don Pablo, and we both invite you. Furthermore . . . by ticket. My dear, we still have classes. (*Laughing.*)

TRIN. Always so amiable !

LUC. And so archæological.

CLARA. Don't be ungrateful to poor Castulo. He showed you through the Mexican saloon before any one. He has nothing in his house reserved from you.

LUC. It's true ; for that reason my gratitude will be eternal.

TRIN. (*growing impatient*). But this Mariana is not coming back.

CLARA. We were told that she had gone out in her carriage for a drive through the Retiro. As she was not receiving to-day . . . and as poor Mariana had been very nervous and very sad, according to what the maid told me . . . she wished, no doubt, to have a little relaxation.

LUC. Mariana is not happy. Ah ! nobody is happy.

TRIN. It is not easy for her to be happy with her temperament. She requires to be married, believe me. She needs a husband of steadiness and judgment to put order into that capricious, irregular, undisciplined brain.

LUC. For that there is nothing like military discipline.

CLARA. As I have been informed by Castulo, who knew her when she was quite a child, . . . she was almost from infancy a very strange creature, and then those family unpleasantnesses

LUC. I have heard something, too. It seems that Mariana's mother . . .

CLARA. That's it.

TRIN. Tell me, tell me.

CLARA. My dear, I know very little—the little that Castulo has told me, and Castulo is not well informed about anything except what took place two thousand years ago. In affairs of the present day he is completely out of his latitude.

TRIN. Still, he must have told you something.

CLARA. It seems that Mariana's mother suffered a good deal from her husband—who was a man of gold !

LUC. That's the way you ladies have of saying that he was a banker.

TRIN. And in the end Mariana's mother . . . eh ?

CLARA. She was very good, very good—an angel.

TRIN. And what more ?

CLARA. Well, Castulo knows no more. For at that time he had to undertake a voyage of exploration to the ruins of Babylon . . or of Troy . . . I don't know which ; he was absent three years, and on his return he found that Mariana's mother had died.

TRIN. And is that all ?

CLARA. Castulo heard something of a scandal, a flight to London, but all in a vague manner. Mariana was eleven years old, and already claimed attention for her divine beauty and her profound sadness. Castulo says that the child was a sweet little Niobe.

TRIN. (*to* LUCIANO). Who was Niobe ?

LUC. Niobe   Niobe . . . Don Castulo has explained that to me several times, but I don't remember. Something about "sorrow petrified."

CLARA. Didn't either of you hear a carriage ? It should be Mariana.

LUC. (*looking towards the garden*). Yes, it is.

Enter MARIANA *from back centre.*

MAR. But, good gracious, why didn't you let me know?

TRIN. Make no apologies.

CLARA. I only thought of coming out at the last moment . . .

MAR. How **are you**, Luciano?

LUC. Always your most obedient.

MAR. I could have no idea that you would come. We made no arrangement last night.

TRIN. People always have a pleasure in being kept waiting at your house.

MAR. God help me! And have you had to wait long?

CLARA. No; half-an-hour at the most.

MAR. You see I was much worried. I was not well. And I went out for the sake of going out. To change my position, as invalids do.

TRIN. But are you ill?

MAR. No, I am not really ill. But—how am I to explain it? . . . The day opened gloomily . . . without light . . . without sun. . . . I need much light, torrents of light. Obscurity—singularly enough . . . makes me nervous. The very opposite of what happens to everybody else.

LUC. So that you would not be able to live in London?

MAR. London! . . . (*Restraining herself.*) Ah! don't speak to me of London. . . . (*With a somewhat forced laugh.*) Unsympathetic, insufferable, odious. Believe me—odious! Oh, that fog! That dulness! Crowded—yet a desert. Great uproar; and in the soul, silence. Much life!—and beside it, death. Oh! I have not re-visited London; I never shall go back to it. (*As if mastered in spite of herself by sorrowful memories.*)

CLARA. When were you there?

MAR. (*as if waking suddenly*). When?   Ah, yes; when I was quite a child.

TRIN. Still, you remember it well.

MAR. The memory of children is prodigious. I

was seven years of age, or not much more : I went back there three years afterwards. But let us not speak of London. (*Changing her tone.*) Let us talk of Italy, of Africa, of Asia. . . . (*Feigning gaiety.*) Listen (*to* CLARA), I am going to rob you of your husband, and he and I shall make a journey, our two selves alone, to the East. Just imagine : I don't know one word of all those antique subjects that he knows from every point of view ; and, nevertheless, be assured that I like them very much. No, Clarita, I must rob you of Castulo, and we shall set out together, the two of us—marching with our faces to the rising sun.

LUC. A good idea, yes !—Steal him from us and take him far, far away.

CLARA. Well, we shall see, we shall see. I don't know whether I shall give my consent ; but to-day I come to ask yours.

MAR. Mine?

CLARA. Yes. Let me explain the diplomatic mission that brings me. I invite you in the name of my husband, and in my own name, to give us your company at breakfast on Sunday. A grand solemnity— connected with the inauguration of our Chamber of Mexican Antiquities. There will be few of us—but all intimate friends; Trinidad, Don Pablo, Luciano. . . .

MAR. (*hesitatingly*). I don't know. . . .

CLARA. Don Joaquin and Daniel.

MAR. (*changing her tone*). Then I accept. With all my life and soul, and I am most heartily obliged to you for your courtesy. Mexican antiquities ! They ought to be very curious.

CLARA. Ask Luciano.

LUC. Ah ! Yes, señora, they are indeed. Very curious.

MAR. And you say on Sunday?

CLARA. Sunday. We are still several days off it: but I was anxious to anticipate, so that you should not accept an engagement elsewhere.

MAR. Sunday, then. The Mexican antiquities!

CLARA. So I have terminated my embassy, and now I retire, in order that Trinidad may deliver her credentials.

MAR. Are you, too, charged with a mission?

TRIN. A very special one. But no, my dear (*to* CLARA), don't go away.

MAR. No; by no means. You shall take a cup of tea, and then you shall stay to dinner with me. Let there be no reply, no discussion.

CLARA. As you please.

LUC. As you please.

MAR. However, you say a mission? And a special mission?

TRIN. And private.

MAR. (*gaily*). That's curious; private!

CLARA. That's why I said we were going to retire. (*Pointing to* LUC.)

LUC. That's why we were retiring.

TRIN. I say no. I shall go with Mariana for a walk round the garden, and we shall there say what we have to talk about. I want a poetic background · the trees, the flowers, the fountains will come to my aid.

MAR. Let it be so, though I don't understand a word. And when we have terminated our conference . . our private conference, we give you notice that we four shall take that little cup of tea in the winter house. Is it agreed?

CLARA. Agreed.

MAR. (*to* TRINIDAD, *taking her arm and turning*

slowly toward the garden). Then let us go there. But are we treating of an affair so solemn, so poetical, and so reserved as you say?

TRIN. You will see.

MAR. Well, I can't guess. . . . (*Aside.*) Only too well.

TRIN. (*mysteriously*). It concerns my brother.

MAR. Ah! . . ˙ A perfect gentleman, and a very good-natured friend.

TRIN. Nothing more?

MAR. We shall terminate the conference in the garden, for otherwise . . . as you already know . . . it will neither be solemn, poetical, nor secret. (*Turning round to* CLARA *and* LUCIANO.) Good-bye for the present. [*Exeunt* MARIANA *and* TRINIDAD.

CLARA. Will Mariana accept?

LUC. No.

CLARA. Why? The general holds a very high position; he is almost in the flower of age. He has great ability and a reputation for bravery. And even what they relate of him, that he gave his first wife her death-blow through jealousy, even that makes him interesting. (*Lowering her voice.*)

LUC. I doubt it: if I were a woman I should never marry an Othello.

CLARA. Then you shouldn't doubt it. If Othello were resuscitated as a widower he would be married within six months. In short, Pablo, with all his apparent coldness, is madly in love with Mariana.

LUC. And with Mariana's riches.

CLARA. With Mariana, with Mariana; let us not always take people from their worst side. And she is mad . . . really mad

LUC. After Daniel.

CLARA. And she shows it by torturing him?

LUC. The one who tortures, loves. Ah! Clarita, torture me!

CLARA (*laughing*). When Castulo lets me have my turn.

LUC. And when will he let you have your turn?

CLARA. I don't know. He is very fond of his Luciano. He says that you have an instinct for Archæology, and a patience . . .

LUC. And on whose account have I so much patience?

CLARA. On mine.

LUC. And by whom am I made to suffer?

CLARA. By him.

LUC. And by whom shall I be driven mad?

CLARA (*laughing*). By him and me.

LUC. But let us not speak of madmen, for here comes Daniel.

CLARA. True; and with his keeper.

SERVANT (*preceding* DON JOAQUIN *and* DANIEL, *who enter*). The Señora is in the garden.

JOAQ. Well; we shall wait here. (*Shaking hands with* CLARA.) How pleased I am to see you!

CLARA. I say the same to you. (*Turning to* DANIEL.) Montoya, my friend . . .

DAN. Always your friend, Clarita.

LUC. A happy meeting, Daniel . . . Don Joaquin. . . . (*Saluting each other.*)

JOAQ. It appears that Mariana is walking among the flowers.

CLARA. Yes, señor.

LUC. One flower more.

DAN. Is she alone?

CLARA. No.

DAN. With whom?

CLARA. With Trinidad.

Luc. A private interview.

Dan. Private?

Clara. So they said.

Joaq. Halloa, halloa!

Clara. What's the matter with you, Daniel? Are you impatient? (Daniel *is incessantly looking toward the garden.*)

Dan. No, señora. Impatient? Why?

Clara. Has your father completely recovered?

Dan. Yes, señora. Many thanks. It was an alarm
. nothing more.

Luc. Does he never come to Madrid?

Dan. Very seldom. He has grown attached to his country-seat, and he never goes out of it. It was the same with him at Seville. He spent two successive years in it. We have there almost an archæological museum, and our Mexican antiquities are not surpassed by those of Don Castulo. My father, also, was very fond of collecting objects of remote date.

Clara (*to* Daniel). You, on the other hand, never leave Madrid; you like objects of recent date.

Joaq. In our youth we like great capitals: it is the passion for busy life. In old age we grow attached to the country: the passion for repose. It is our mother earth that calls us. The foliage moved by the breeze, the stream curled by the foam, the sun piercing through the leaves and falling on the grass in circles of light, seem, as it were, the smiles and caresses of the general mother who says to her children: " Come to me, child with the white hair, for I have made ready thy cradle of earth."

Clara. Don't say sad things, Don Joaquin.

Luc. Between Don Castulo with his Archæology, you with your eternal elegy, and Daniel with his melancholy   the truth is that one feels in an agony.

CLARA. Ave Maria!

JOAQ. But really I am not saying sad things.

CLARA. They must be sad, for look how Daniel is. He never takes his eyes away from the garden.

LUC. It is his mother earth which calls him. And if it is not mother earth, it must be mother nature.

CLARA. Don't be so unpleasantly insinuating.

SERVANT (*entering*). The mistress says that you may pass on when you please to the winter-house: tea is ready.   [*Exit.*

CLARA. Shall we go there, Luciano?

LUC. With you I would go. . . . I'll not say to that delicious garden, but to the Mexican Hall of Don Castulo.

CLARA (*to* DON JOAQUIN *and* DANIEL). Are you coming?

JOAQ. Excuse me: I also have to speak privately to Mariana, and I shall wait for her here.

CLARA. This is the day of private conferences. Shall I announce it to Mariana?

JOAQ. If you will be so good. . . .

CLARA. With my friends I am always so. (*Goes toward the back with* LUCIANO.)

LUC. (*as he is going out*). And must we not confer in all secrecy?

CLARA. It must be briefly, for they are awaiting us.

LUC. A brief spell of passion.   [*Exeunt.*

DAN. (*to* JOAQUIN). Are you going to say something to Mariana? You will not desist from your project?

JOAQ. No. My resolution is irrevocable.

DAN. Then let it be so. Lend me the strength in

which I am myself wanting. (*Falls on a chair.* JOA-
QUIN *approaches him affectionately.*)

JOAQ. I love you as if you were my own son. You
were the comrade, the friend, almost the brother of
my poor Fernando. My poor Fernando! . . . And
on his death-bed he said to me: "Take care of
Daniel. His father is so infirm, that he is as though
he did not exist. Now that he has no father, you
must be one to him." And I am so.

DAN. A father: a friend: an angel that always
comes to save me.

JOAQ. An angel of seventy years! And with
countless white hairs! But, after all, the angels in
heaven, though without white hairs, are still older.
Mariana is your bad angel. I shall be your good
angel.

DAN. No: there is no badness in Mariana.
Make me out to be what you please, Mariana is not
wicked.

JOAQ. I know what Mariana is: I have been
acquainted with her for many years. Yes, at heart
she is good, noble, high-spirited, pure; but with all
her goodness she is dangerous. One of those women
who unhinge a brain; who make a heart bound; who
receive every morning an amorous kiss from the
goddess of madness; who approach you bearing in
one hand happiness, in the other despair, and no one
knows—they themselves are ignorant of it—which
hand they will give you.

DAN. But she loves me?

JOAQ. I don't know. I think so; but I don't know.

DAN. Then if she loves me, let vertigo, madness,
despair come upon me . . . what does it matter!
But let her tell me so, let me know it and I shall
never complain.

JOAQ. How you do go on! Poor Daniel!

DAN. See, Don Joaquin, this doubt it is that is killing me. At times I feel impulses to press the pretty neck of Mariana between my strong hands, to feel the final contractions of her lips, to drink her last breath, and to think—"Ah! she has not died without kissing me." No, don't say anything: I already know that these are ravings of madness.

JOAQ. No; I am truly glad that you should speak to me in such fashion. For this day must decide all. You shall either be married prosaically to her, or you must keep away from her for ever.

DAN. I be separated from her? Never.

JOAQ. You are a man, and will have to bear your-self as a man of character and of heart. Either be with her, as absolute lord and master, or at a great distance from her; (*angrily*) for it isn't pleasant to see you suffering so. But, gently: I also have my temper, and I can afford to speak sternly to Mariana. For that woman, you must know, is under obligation to listen to me. Ho, ho there! (*Looking toward the garden as if to challenge* MARIANA.) You know the history of her family?

DAN. I have known her a year, and it seems as though I had known her all my life. As for her family, what have I to do with it?

JOAQ. Well, in her family history there have been very dark days: and in those days I was at the side of little Mariana . . and also by the side of her mother. . . . Come, I tell you that she must hear me, that she must respect me, and, if her temper were not such as it is, I might almost say that she will have to obey me.

DAN. She? She will not obey.

JOAQ. No? I say she will be agitated with her

little alarms at this very moment. If Clara tells her that I am waiting for her, and that we must have a talk together, she will not be so very easy in her mind, eh? What will you bet that she leaves the others and comes in search of me? I tell you that inside that pretty little head there dances this idea with its co-responsive little trembling : " Why should Don Joaquin want to speak to me?" (*Laughing in anticipation of the terror which he attributes to* MARIANA.) She is afraid of me,—ah !—she is afraid of me.

DAN. She is afraid of nobody: neither shall she be afraid of anybody. For am not I here to defend her? (*Passionately.*)

JOAQ. See how he flies out! You are a poor creature, and a fool into the bargain. You were not so once, but you are now. Do you know how the first fool in the world was manufactured? Well, he was formed out of a lover—that's very simple. The lover placed himself before the object of his tender longings ; and, it is clear, he remained like a block-head, without saying a word but—" I love you so much (= *tanto*). I love you so much, I love you so much." And by force of this repetition of " tanto, tanto, tanto," . . . the result was " tonto "[1] (= *a fool*).

DAN. Do you observe that she isn't coming? (*Looking towards the garden.*)

JOAQ. (*looking also : then, after a pause*). Do you observe that she is coming? . . . Didn't I say so?

---

[1] Señor Echegaray suffers from chronic attacks of the punning rabies. What is the quality of his puns may be judged from the above melancholy example. It is to be regretted that a man who shows an undeniable sense of humour through much of his work, should lower himself to this most witless of all methods of arousing laughter.

Now you shall see, now you shall see how I'll tame the pretty little wild animal.   And do you go at once to the garden, plant yourself before the first trunk of a tree you meet, fancy it's Mariana, and until I give you notice to, stop, keep on repeating "tanto." . . . . I should say "tonto, tonto, tonto!" . . . Eh, quick!

DAN. How beautiful! . . .

JOAQ. Will you or will you not let me have a clear field?

DAN. Yes: you are right: this must come to an end.   [*Exit to the left of the garden.*

JOAQ. Now we shall see, little Mariana!   I am going to fight a pitched battle with you.   Ah! heart of gold, temper of iron, head of a bird; you must now understand from Don Joaquin that you are not going to kill my Daniel.

Enter MARIANA.

MAR. (*showing extraordinary affection*).   My dear Don Joaquin!   My father! . . . Why did you not come to where I was?   (*Looking around.*)   And Daniel?   Was he tired of waiting for me?   Why did you not come forward?   (*Lets herself fall on a sofa or cushioned seat.*)   To-day I feel sad, depressed. . . . I don't know how . . . and I'm glad to see at my side my good friends. . . . You and Daniel are the friends of my predilection.   But you know that already.

JOAQ. Oh yes; now come your caresses.   You are now acting the part of the spoiled child—I know you.

MAR. (*sadly and somewhat caressingly*).   I should think you do know me!—For many years.

JOAQ. I have not come to listen to your coaxings: I come to speak seriously to you.

MAR. Everybody wants to speak seriously to-day. To-day when I needed gaiety, rejoicing, liveliness,

pleasant conversation, playful friendship — to-day
every one must wear the face of an ambassador or a
schoolmaster. (*With a kind of sad, wheedling fretfulness.*)

JOAQ. Let us take it that I wear the face of a
schoolmaster. Listen to me.

MAR. Speak : I shall listen humbly.

JOAQ. That's what I want from you : humility. Do
you ever make an examination of conscience?

MAR. (*with merry surprise*). I?

JOAQ. Answer me.

MAR. Yes, señor; from time to time.

JOAQ. And what does your conscience tell you—
that you are good, or that you are bad ?

MAR. You make me laugh . . . and I have no
wish to do so.

JOAQ. Answer me !

MAR. My conscience speaks to me in so confused
a manner that I find it hard to understand it. Moreover, I interrogate it when I am about to go to sleep ;
and I being half asleep, and it not being very wide-
awake, I neither know what I am asking it, nor does
it know well what to answer me. And thus we stand.

JOAQ. Good: then I shall question it.

MAR. Poor little conscience ! . . . (*Coaxingly.*)
Let it go to sleep.

JOAQ. It must not be. And let us talk seriously.
Mariana, I know that you are not bad at heart. But
towards Daniel you behave like a woman without
heart and without conscience.

MAR. Don Joaquin ! . . . I ? . . . In what way?

JOAQ. You know. Either you love him, or you
don't love him. If the former, you should not torture
him. If the latter, you should take away all hope
from him.

MAR. But what do you say? That I torture him?

JOAQ. There, now—at this very moment you are not only wicked, you are hypocritical. You know that you martyr him without compassion : and that you delight in his martyrdom.

MAR. (*energetically*). It is true.

JOAQ. Thank God you confess it. And why do you do so?

MAR. How can I tell? No doubt because I am wicked. But the fault isn't all mine. Others have made me what I am. I was good when I was a child. I felt within me immense treasures of tenderness. Always compassionate, always affectionate. I was like a little honeycomb full of the sweetest honey : others robbed the comb of its honey and refilled the cells with bitterness. Is it my fault if, when my heart is wrung, it distils gall? (*Pressing her bosom.*) I did not put it here ; let the complaint be directed against the one who placed it within me.

JOAQ. Poor Mariana ; in that you are right.

MAR. When I was very little, what did I see in my home? A struggle, implacable, secret, cruel, between my father and my mother. My father. . I don't know ; but, from the words which I heard falling from the servants, this idea took root within me—"that my father was bad." At first I was afraid of him : then I left off loving him : later he inspired me with repulsion : in the end I looked upon him with indifference. My father regarded indifferently by me, and I being only eight years of age ! What can be expected from a well-spring which hardly begins to flow when it is dried up?

JOAQ. In all this you are right. But, on the other hand, your mother. . . .

MAR. Of my mother I was very fond : I loved her

always, and if I could requite on any one the wrong that was done to her. . . . Oh ! the retribution should not be unaccomplished for want of wishing. And nevertheless   there did come a day   when I became afraid of my mother also   You know it. (*Remains pensive.*)

JOAQ. Go on, Mariana. This conference is decisive for you. I know the events of your life : I don't know the history of your heart.

MAR. And you would like to know among what briars and brambles it was left to be torn to pieces ? Isn't that so ?

JOAQ. Precisely. (*A group is visible in the garden* —TRINIDAD, CLARA, *and* LUCIANO—*then they disappear.*)

MAR. Well, let us go on.—But (*approaching the back of the stage*), will anybody hear us ?

JOAQ. They were coming this way, but they saw us wrapped up in our conversation and they have become wrapped up in the thicket. (*They return to the first wing,* MARIANA *pensive,* DON JOAQUIN *contemplating her.*) Won't you continue ? Come . . . tell me of your impressions : the incidents I already know.

MAR. And did you know Don Felix Alvarado ? With what delight (*Terrible irony.*) I pronounce that name and bite that name ! (*Biting her lips.*)

JOAQ. And why bite, eh ? . . . I did not know him, you little savage.

MAR. Well, he was gallant, sympathetic, affectionate, somewhat melancholy. I don't know from where he came : I think from America. He seemed rich : I don't know if he was so : he lent much money to my father. How respectful towards my mother ! how affectionate towards me !

JOAQ. I have heard of all that : be brief.

MAR. You desired that we should have an examina-tion of conscience. It is good that you should know how I have suffered, in order that you may under-stand what a delight I take at times in making other people suffer.

JOAQ. But how is poor Daniel to blame?

MAR. It's true. Poor Daniel! (*Pensively.*)

JOAQ. Get done.

MAR. Listen. I was eight years old . . . it must have been two or three o'clock in the morning. . . . I was sleeping in my crib, and I dreamed that I was giving a great many kisses to my doll, because it had called me "mamma." The doll soon began to kiss me in return, but so fiercely that it caused me pain : and the doll became very large : and it was my mother and she was holding me in her arms : and I .   I was not sleeping now : it was no dream : I was awake. Behind my mother was a man standing it was Alvarado who was saying : " Come !" and my mother said · " No, not without her ! " And he said : " What the devil . . . then, with her ! " Afterwards there seemed another dream : a nightmare : some-thing that whirls round and oppresses. My mother, dressing me as one may dress a lunatic or a doll, with shaking, with pulling, almost with blows. And Alvarado, in a stifled voice, pressing her : " Quick, quick, make haste ! " I have never undergone a sensation like it. It was trivial, it was grotesque— but it was horrible. She could not succeed in getting the little socks on me ; she could not manage to button my boots ; my drawers were reversed ; the petticoats left with the opening at the side ; my dress half loose, although I was saying : " It requires to be fastened, it requires to be fastened." But Alvarado was still repeating : " Quick, quick, make haste, make haste ! " Then a cloak of my mother's fastened round my body : then a hat-ribbon that was strangling me tied round my head : then my mother snatched me up in her arms : then we entered a carriage that went very fast, and then I heard a kiss and I thought : " But, my God, for whom was it, for whom was it ?— nobody has kissed me." Ah ! my own mother, my own mother ! . . . (*Bursts into tears.*)

JOAQ. Enough now.

MAR. No : you wished for an examination of conscience ? Then we shall have an examination of conscience. A general confession ? A general confession, then, you shall hear. You wanted to know what others have made of me ? Well, now you know it. You wished to know why I believe in nobody . . . except in you . . . and now you know that, too. Let me go on to the end. We went to London. What a life, my God, what a life ! My mother cried bitterly in Madrid : but she cried more in London. I always looked on with eyes wide open : I understood something, and I never cried. My mother was very good. I say that she was very good ! That man was infamous and coarse. How many times before me has he made her put on gay dresses, laces, and jewels ; but brutally, amid blows and curses, by force—as my mother had dressed me that night ! And again, when Alvarado went on enveloping my mother in her shroud, in the shroud of orgie, there sounded a kiss ; but that kiss was for me ; it was one which my mother gave me amid sobs and tears when that man tore her away to himself, and left me alone with the gloomy fretfulness of a silkworm stifled in sepulchral rottenness.

JOAQ. No more, no more !

MAR. At last, weariness, desertion, misery, hunger,

death . . . my mother in her agony . . . I in the
street . . . I went to you . . . you were very kind
and good . . . but indeed you have not suffered as
Mariana has suffered. (*Leans her head upon the
breast of* DON JOAQUIN *and embraces him while
weeping.*)

JOAQ. Yes, poor Mariana ; I buried your mother ;
I took you to myself : I brought you to Spain : I
gave you up to your father . . . and you were
happy.

MAR. Happy ! . . . Courteous indifference : insipid
luxury : the respect of servants for their monthly
wages : my father always far away : the governess
always close at hand : my mother nevermore anywhere ! I like to suffer, but I like to have enjoy-
ment. Let sorrow come in torrents, if it bring a drop
—though it be no more than one drop—of love. Ah !
how I missed those kisses in London, with all their
tears and all their impurities.

JOAQ. God help me, child. I wish I had been able
to tear all these records from your memory.

MAR. Then my wedding ! (*Laughing ironically.*)
We have not spoken of my wedding. " This is your
husband," says my father to me, and gives me a
portrait. I look at it : I think it agreeable. " Good,
I'll be married   " " He is very rich . . . "
" Better still," I say. We get married by power of
attorney : I am taken to Cuba : I land : I am met
by some ladies dressed in black ; there's no wedding,
there is mourning. (*Indifferently.*) So much for that !
My loving husband had died from the results of a
duel about a ballet dancer. One more illusion ! And
with the same passion that I had said, " Good, I'll be
married," I said, " Good, I am a widow." What
would you have me to be, Don Joaquin ? What

would you have me to care for? In what or in whom would you have me to believe? In men? Why? Because they are like my father, like Alvarado, like my husband? No ; let them suffer; let them weep ; let them die !

JOAQ. Daniel is not so ; he does not deserve what's merited by others.

MAR. He seems not to be so now ; but who knows what he will be ! Alvarado, too, was tender-natured, and he did not display himself truly until he had killed my mother. Daniel has not yet shed tears ; at least I have not seen him weep. I have seen Alvarado shed tears . . . in the beginning. My husband died for the sake of another little wife than me. Daniel has not yet died for his Mariana. Let him do that . (*With profound irony and cruel laughter.*) and then we shall see.

JOAQ. No, you shall do nothing of that sort with Daniel, you little wild beast! I'll pair your claws and wrench your teeth out ! Do you wish to make Daniel Montoya pay for the faults of Felix Alvarado? Well, he shall not pay for them. I now see what you are, and I am sorry for it, I am sorry for it. I did wrong to pick you out of the refuse of London.

MAR. Don Joaquin !

JOAQ. Because you have stumbled against evil, everything is bad? Walk along a marshy soil and you will sink into the mire. But spring aside, go further on, and you will come upon valleys with flowers, woods with shade, mountains with snow, horizons with light.

MAR. Who could do that?

JOAQ. If you remain in the swampy ground, the fault is your own. March on. Come, now, you most obstinate creature: are there no good people in the world ? Was not your mother good . . . in spite of all ?

MAR. (*with anguish, clinging to* DON JOAQUIN). Yes.

JOAQ. Were not you good when you were little ?

MAR. I was.

JOAQ. What the devil——! Am not I good?

MAR. My God ! I should think so.

JOAQ. Then why should not Daniel be so?

MAR. Let him prove it.

JOAQ. Well, that will be easy.

MAR. How?

JOAQ. By your marrying him.

MAR. (*archly*). Then he wants to marry me?

JOAQ. Yes ; he has that much bad taste. For your sake he has rejected   . it's a fact, word of honour . . a young girl . . . younger than you, (*With evident exaggeration.*) for she is only eighteen years old, and prettier than you, and richer than you, and better tempered than you. You now see the madness that this madman has been guilty of for your sake.

MAR. (*coldly*). Then he has done wrong. Although, look you, if he likes me better than that person—in spite of her being so young, so lovely, so rich, and so good—he has done well.

JOAQ. You would have been sorry if he had married her? Come, the truth ; say what you think, and don't tell me a lie.

MAR. (*after a pause*). Yes.

JOAQ. Then you love him?

MAR. It is not impossible ; but I don't know.

JOAQ. Then you'll have to know ; and if you don't love him, you must bid him good-bye for ever.

MAR. (*with irony in which there is something of conviction*). Why ? If he is happy at my side, if he

is happy in his suffering, and I am happy in making
him suffer, why should we be separated?

JOAQ. (*angrily*). Because a man such as he is
was not born to be a plaything for anybody—not even
for you.

MAR. (*rather coquettishly*). Am I so good for
nothing?

JOAQ. He is a great deal better than you. There
(*very ill at ease*), coquetries are of no avail with me.

MAR. (*caressingly*). What a bad temper you are
in with your Mariana to-day!

JOAQ. Pah! Seriously, and for the last time: you
shall either be his wife, or I'll take him off to Madrid
to find the girl, eighteen years old, and with eighteen
million pesetas of income.

MAR. I shall neither be his wife, nor will you take
him away.

JOAQ. No?

MAR. No. I am no longer a child. (*Jestingly and
laughing defiantly*).

JOAQ. (*going to the door of the garden*). We shall
see. . . . Daniel!   . Daniel!

MAR. (*with a certain emotion*). Are you calling
him?

JOAQ. As you now see. Daniel! . . .

MAR. But for God's sake, don't call him yet! . . .
We have not finished our conference.   We must
find a *modus vivendi*. . . . (*Laughing.*) Isn't that
what you call it?

JOAQ. Daniel! . . . Come . . . it's you I'm calling.

MAR. (*with ill-concealed emotion*). How you do go
on to-day!

Enter DANIEL.

DAN. Mariana!   (*restraining himself.*)
Señora! . . .

MAR. Good-day to you, Daniel.

JOAQ. (*to* DANIEL). I have done for you what a father would not have done for his son : I'll say more, I have done for both of you all that I could ; and I can do no more. (*To* DANIEL.) If you will follow my advice you'll take a final farewell of Mariana. (*To* MARIANA.) If you will obey my command—and I have some sort of a right to command you—undeceive him and never see him again. I have spoken as a man of heart, and a man of honour also, speaks to two persons whom he really loves, but who are not in their senses. Think of what I have said, or don't think of it : I have finished : make up your minds : shall be curious to see how two lunatics make up their minds. Untie the knot if you can : if you can't, twist it round your necks very tight. Good-bye for the present ; I am going to take tea . . . no ; an ice.

MAR. But, Don Joaquin !

JOAQ. Two ices !

DAN. Don Joaquin !

JOAQ. A dozen of ices ! . . . Good-bye. . . . They love each other ; they will come to an understanding.

                                           [*Exit.*

MAR. (*seating herself with an air of weariness*). He is vexed because, according to him, I torment you ; I make you unhappy : I ought not to see you any more (*sadly*).

DAN. No, Mariana ; torment me without mercy, but don't forbid me to see you.

MAR. (*as before, sad and caressing*). Don Joaquin says that I am very cruel.

DAN. What does it matter? If I am the one who suffers, and if I like to go on suffering, what right have other people to thrust themselves in the way ?

MAR. Are you anxious that we should be good

friends? I shall be very affectionate towards you, and I'll never be cruel . if, indeed, I am so at present, of which I am not very well convinced.

Dan. No. Friends? No. I prefer that we should be as we are : I loving you and telling you so ; you hating me, making me endure martyrdom, and from time to time allowing me to have a glimmer of hope, though I know it to be false. Let us go on as we are, go on as we are : I can still bear more misery, and if you take a delight in my suffering, you may torture me still further.

Mar. (*impatiently*). But, my God! how unjust you all are towards me. Why, then, I am a monster, a Sphinx, I suppose !

Dan. But I don't complain. For what are all the fibres of my heart if not that you may pluck from them sweet or mournful notes? It is as you please. What happiness ! You don't feel a delight in torment-ing any one else than me ! Therefore I must be in your eyes that which others are not. And what I long for is that you should not treat me as you do others. You favour Don Pablo with much respect, great consideration, courteous phrases. . . . And as for me? It is : " Come here, Daniel : throw yourself at my feet like a dog : suffer, weep, writhe, go mad, die !" Two beings may become intertwined, com-mingled with one another by love or by hatred. Can it not be love? Good ; then let it be hatred. Let me feel my Mariana near me, tearing my heart out with her sweet little hands, setting my soul in flames with her eyes, drinking in with rapture the sight of my agony ! But near me, near me, not far away. Separate us? Never, Mariana !

Mar. But, God save me ! I am not the woman you suppose. I cannot love . . . because I cannot love.

I have been very unhappy, and the fountain of all tenderness, of all confidence, has been dried up within me. I feel no love : I feel no tenderness ; and I don't want to feel them. To deliver up the soul is to lose it ; it is flinging it to the contempt or the indifference of others. Because if I said to you : "Well, then, I love you, I accept you, I shall be your wife," I should scarcely have finished saying so when you would care for me less, and then less, and in the end not at all. "She is mine ! Good-bye to passion, to delirium, to self-deception." When I seem to laugh at you, I am not laughing at you : it is that I laugh while thinking : "Poor Daniel ! why, he does not imagine that he loves me much. What a joke if I told him so !"

DAN. (*striking his breast*). What passes within here, you don't know.

MAR. Yes, Daniel : we are all created after the same fashion. If I ever came to feel for you a true passion—what madness, what shame, what despair ! (*She visibly struggles with the affection which she is feeling for* DANIEL.)

DAN. Despair] perhaps ; but there's the happiness. Do you not understand ? have you never tasted with relish the bliss of suffering ? Then I am happier than you. Indifference, disrelish, frivolity, always all the same, a perennial half-tint, a monotonous sound, a somnolent limbo that, that is despair and death. Is it so you live, Mariana ? Then you are more unfortunate than I.

MAR. It's the truth : that is indeed the truth.

DAN. Try, for once in your life, what it is to love and to suffer. Love me, Mariana. I ask it now for your sake ; not for myself, for you. And if you have a doubt of me, all the better : you will love me more. And the greater your doubts and anxieties, the greater will be your delights. And if you think that you must lose me for ever—ah! then your love will be infinite.

MAR. That would be a curious probation, Daniel.

DAN. If we love from the inmost soul, the insubstantial world that surrounds us disappears, and our love creates a new world. I see you in all parts, and I feel love for you in all its forms. Sometimes the tenderness of a father: who contemplates his Mariana with pride and with respect: caresses her as a little child: presses her hand in all gentleness: puts back in its place a disordered curl: kisses her on the forehead.

MAR. Poor Daniel! . . . And poor me! I never had a father who loved me in that fashion.

DAN. At other times I feel towards you a fraternal affection: the calm and joyous fondness of a friend and a companion. And I put my arm around your waist, and you throw your arm about my neck, and we run among God's own fields, playing as if we were two boys. And if you saw what lively fellows we are!

MAR. How good you are! And what an evil fate is mine! . . . I never had a brother with whom I could play in such a manner as you speak of.

DAN. Sometimes . . . this indeed is rare! . . . I don't know how, but I am your husband, and we have a hearth and a family and a homely corner for ourselves. And time flies upon the wings of angels, even until we are old! You see what are the whims of the imagination!

MAR. (*laughing*). They are indeed whims.—And what do we do?

DAN. Well, I die of pure old age: and you, who are also very old, embrace me amidst your tears

and I, as one in dreams, hear you saying : " For my
Daniel in life : for my Daniel in death." Your tears
roll down the furrows formed by my wrinkles, as
mourning through a valley of tears : and your white
curls fall upon my shrivelled lips : and my soul
escapes from death—from death with its visage so
foul and its scythe, which was bearing it away—to
return to the lips and to kiss for the last time those
white curls, as it kissed the black curls of its
Mariana.

MAR. (*much moved and drying her eyes*). What an
imagination ! . . . (*With coquetry.*) But these curls,
you see, are still black.

DAN. But they will be white ; and who will kiss
them if I be not the man ?

MAR. And why must you not be?

DAN. Because you'll not have it so.

MAR. Bah ! I have said nothing.—And have you
done with your imaginations ?

DAN. No. Many times I am neither father, nor
brother, nor friend, nor venerable spouse ; I am your
impassioned Daniel. And I am very close to you,
and you do not push me away. (*Approaching her.*)

MAR. Good ; then I shall not push you away. . . .
But it's through curiosity—nothing more.

DAN. And I grasp your hand ; (*seizes it*) not with
the gentle pressure of the father or the brother ; but
to squeeze it desperately ; to martyrise it.

MAR. No (*laughing, but evidently much moved*) :
why it does not hurt me even yet.

DAN. It is because you have no feeling.

MAR. In real truth, no. But here ends the dream
. . . for it has all been a dream   . and we must
awake. (*Draws away her hand.*)

DAN. I was going to tell you what was said to me

in those dreams or in those imaginations by Mariana
the Mariana of my delusions.

MAR. I shall suppose it, without your repeating it.

DAN. And you won't repeat it?

MAR. Repeat all that she says ! No . . . it would
compromise me.

DAN. Well, only one thing.

MAR. Which? If it is not much—granted.

DAN. Don't say that you love—say that you will
try me, to see if you can love me. (*A pause.*)

MAR. (*resolutely*). I will try you.

DAN. Say, moreover, that if you don't succeed in
loving me, you will love no one else.

MAR. You, or nobody.

DAN. Not Don Pablo !

MAR. Don Pablo ! What a child you are ! (*She
rises laughing.* DANIEL *rises also, and* DON
JOAQUIN *enters without being heard by them.*)

DAN. The fact is, if you love another man
swear it by my salvation . . . if you love another . . .

MAR. Yes ; I know already. (*In tragi-comic
tones.*) You'll kill me : and you'll kill him.

DAN. (*seizing her hand*). As there is a God that
hears us !

MAR. You are now really hurting me.

DAN. But is the compact made?

MAR. Made and sealed. And if you squeeze me
a little harder it will be sealed with blood.

JOAQ. (*advancing*). Have you made a compact?

MAR. And we have a witness; for you appear like
an apparition.

JOAQ. I shall be one.

Enter, laughing, CLARA, TRINIDAD, *and* LUCIANO.

CLARA. And should any more witnesses be wanting, here are we.

:. as one in dreams, bear you saying: "For my
al n : fe : for my Daniel in death." Your tears
•- :he furrows formed by my wrinkles, as
sang :hrough a valley of tears: and your white

spes !- -; death—from death with its visage so
. 's s-ythe, which was bearing it away—to
• : e:;s and to kiss for the last time those
s. as it kissed the black curls of its

—b. à married and drying her eyes). What an
actress ' . . . (With coquetry.) But these curls,
. . . will black.
• they will be white; and who will kiss
. . . the man?
You ur must you not be?
: . . .:s you'll not have it so.
. . . ' I have said nothing.—And have you
. . . . imaginations?
. . 'Many times I am neither father, nor
mother, nor friend, nor venerable spouse; I am your
beloved Daniel. And I am very close to you,
do not push me away. (Approaching her.)
w . . !; then I shall not push you away. . . .
. . .gh curiosity—nothing more.
And I grasp your hand; (seizes it) not with
. . . pressure of the father or the brother; but
squeeze it desperately; to martyrise it.
. . . . nothing, but evidently much moved):
. . not hurt me even yet.
•. . because you have no feeling
:n real truth, no. But here en
. has all been a dream . .
' . . .s away her hand.)
• was going to tell you what was

those dreams or in those imaginations by Mariana
. . the Mariana of my delusions.

MAR. I shall suppose it, without your repeating it.

DAN. And you won't repeat it?

MAR. Repeat all that she says! No . . . it would
compromise me.

DAN. Well, only one thing.

MAR. Which? If it is not much—granted.

DAN. Don't say that you love—say that you will
try me, to see if you can love me. (*A pause.*)

MAR. (*resolutely*). I will try you.

DAN. Say, moreover, that if you don't succeed in
loving me, you will love no one else.

MAR. You, or nobody.

DAN. Not Don Pablo!

MAR. Don Pablo! What a child you are! (*She
rises laughing.* DANIEL *rises also, and* DON
JOAQUIN *enters without being heard by them.*)

DAN. The fact is, if you love another man . . I
swear it by my salvation . . . if you love another . . .

MAR. Yes; I know already. (*In tragic
tones.*) You'll kill me: and you'll kill him.

DAN. (*seizing her hand*). As there is a God that
hears us!

MAR. You are now really hurting me.

DAN. But is the compact made?

MAR. Made and sealed. And if you squeeze me
a little harder it will be sealed with blood.

JOAQ. (*advancing*). Have you made a compact?

MAR. And we have a witness; for you appear like
an apparition.

JOAQ. I shall be one.

Enter, laughing, CLARA, TRINIDAD, *and Luisa.*

CLARA. And should any more witnesses be wanting, here are we.

LUC. All of us.

TRIN. All.   But what is it about?

JOAQ. A secret compact.

DAN. (*to* MARIANA). You renew it?

MAR. (*giving him her hand*). In presence of all I ratify it.

DAN. Our lives are bound up in it.

MAR. Be it so.   (*They remain with clasped hands.*)

JOAQ. What an opportunity, if I bore a sacerdotal character! (*Acting as if he showered benedictions on them.*)

MAR. (*laughing*). With a benediction nothing is lost, is it not true, dear?   (*To* TRINIDAD.)

DAN. With a benediction everything is gained. (*They remain with hands clasped:* DON JOAQUIN *blessing them; the others laughing around them.*)

END OF ACT II.

ACT III.

The scene represents a hall in the house of DON
CASTULO. *This hall is approached by two or
three saloons, whether in front of it, whether in
converging lines, but in such fashion that they are
partly visible. In them all are displayed artistic
and archæological objects, bronzes, earthenware,
carpets, pictures, statues, &c. In the stage
decoration, whatever is exposed seems so from
choice, nothing has the character of being brought
forward through necessity of filling up. It will
be proper to create a special atmosphere, as it
were, for the entire act, and there need be no
limitation of form or adornment to bring about
this result. It must be remembered that this is
the house of* DON CASTULO.

TIME—Day.

Enter CLARA and DON PABLO.

CLARA. Then you are tired of seeing antiquities?
PABLO. I am for the modern. My taste for what's
ancient is concentrated on the army. And in the
matter of age, I shall have enough with what awaits
me. I like the youthful, the new, what brings with
it the lights of morning and the joys of dawn.

71

CLARA. That's why you are so fond of Mariana.

PABLO. That's why; and because she is Mariana.

CLARA. I am indiscreet in speaking to you of our good and most beautiful friend.

PABLO. You are never indiscreet—least of all when speaking of her.

CLARA. Very good, very beautiful—is she not? but with very little judgment.

PABLO. Nobody has judgment; do you not remark that in all creation there is only one day of judgment —the Judgment Day.

CLARA (*laughing*). And that's why they tell us it's the final judgment—the first and the Last.

PABLO. Well, now you see. Do I, for example, rejoice in the possession of judgment? And that, though I am already far enough advanced in years to be judicious; but not so far advanced as to afford me the right not to be so. At fifteen years of age one has no judgment: at forty-eight it should be a law of necessity: at sixty-eight it may be dispensed with—if there is any left to make use of.

CLARA. So you are not judicious?

PABLO. No, señora.

CLARA. Why?

PABLO. Trinidad has already told you, and it is no mystery. I sought the hand of Mariana, in spite of your counsels and warnings; with courteous words she declined the honour which, as she said, I was bestowing upon her.

CLARA. And what follows?

PABLO. That I'll not desist. At this very moment my sister should be speaking to Don Joaquin upon the subject. I am driven back, and I return to the assault. Every one says that Mariana will be married to Daniel; and I don't believe it. My mother was a Navarrese, my father was from Aragon, and I am a prodigy of stubbornness.

CLARA. All this proves you to be a man in love.

PABLO. It is the way I act, at any rate.

CLARA. So that you don't forswear hopes of Mariana?

PABLO. No, señora.

CLARA. And if you should be conquered?

PABLO. And if I should be the conqueror?

CLARA (*laughing*). Then you will know what has to be done. But let us conceive the worse case—if you should be conquered.

PABLO. The man who is the vanquished to-day is the victor to-morrow. I am forty-eight years old: I can wait for fifteen more;—in ten years Troy was taken.

CLARA (*laughing*). You are Homeric.

PABLO. Not altogether so. A woman is not a fortified city.

CLARA. One woman, Helen, fled to that fortified city.

PABLO. And in the end Menelaus recovered her, and returned home with her.

CLARA. And so little as that would content you?

PABLO. No: our classical traditions would not permit me to be so stupidly good-natured as were those heroes. To resistance I oppose determination; to beauty—submission; for treason, I reserve the salutary lessons due from one who is *the physician of his own honour.*[1] (*With a forced laugh.*)

CLARA. Now you are tragic.

PABLO. Now, and always, I am a man of honour, in love with one woman, and ambitious to give her his name.

CLARA. Whatever may fall out?

[1] The reference is to Calderon's drama, "El Medico de su honra." The italics are Señor Echegaray's.

Pablo. Whatever may fall out.

Clara. No fear of rivals?

Pablo. No fear of any one.

Clara. Resolved to conquer?

Pablo. Resolved to struggle.

Clara. That's how I like men to be.

Pablo. As Mariana is, so do I like women to be. And as you are . . . (*with much courtesy*) so I like wives to be.

Clara. Here come Trinidad and Don Joaquin, and from the faces that they wear, I don't think the conference has brought forth satisfactory results.

Pablo. It was not likely to bring them forth. But no matter.

Enter Trinidad *and* Don Joaquin.

Clara (*to* Joaquin). What do you think of my husband's collections?

Joaq. They ought to possess great merit; but I am not a person to give an authoritative opinion.

Clara. Don Joaquin is like Don Pablo; he does not like what's old.

Joaq. Weaknesses of old age—isn't that so, Don Pablo?

Pablo. I have no weaknesses yet.

Joaq. I have many.

Clara *and* Don Joaquin *form one group:* Trinidad *and* Don Pablo *form another apart.*

Pablo. What does he say?

Trin. That he is neither the father nor the guardian of Mariana.

Pablo. In other words—that he declares war against us?

Trin. That's what I told him.

PABLO. And what did he answer?

TRIN. That war ought to be very agreeable to such a valiant soldier as you.

PABLO. So it is. That's well. We shall see.

CLARA. Here comes Mariana: I'm sure that she at least has been delighted with the knick-knacks of my husband.

Enter, by a different door from the others, MARIANA, DON CASTULO, *and* LUCIANO.

MAR. Beyond all price! Admirable! . . . My God, what a collection! . Don Castulo, your house is an enchanted palace.

CAST. You have great intellect. There are no more than two persons here who have what we might call the "Archæological spirit": Mariana and Luciano.

JOAQ. Luciano too?

CAST. Luciano is already a master.

CLARA. A master! I thought he had not gone further than the advanced pupil.

CAST. A master. He becomes ecstatic when listening to me : he does not dare to breathe.

LUC. No, sir, I do not.

PABLO. So all these antiquities please you very much?

MAR. Very much, Don Pablo. With what delight I could live in this house! But alone, completely alone. How I should walk at nightfall through these rooms! And these wonderful objects involved in the approaching and extending gloom! And the last gleams of twilight extracting, from here and there, lost reflections, fugitive scintillations, sudden splendours .. now from a steel helmet, now from a poniard, a remnant of brocade, a garment of purple, a lamp of bronze or an Arabic plate. What thoughts would be mine! What subjects I should discuss! What histories, what dramas! And without knowing anything of it all: mingling all: confusing all. A ghost-like morion from the gallery, a glory that comes down from the last light of heaven, one fragment or another of earthenware, of iron, of cloth, the refuse of the destructive centuries of old. With that I should be content.

LUC. Well, I should not.

MAR. Come, Don Castulo, I envy you all this: if I could, I should rob you of your treasure.

CAST. (*in a tone of triumph, and turning to the others*). What do you think of that?

LUC. We all envy you your treasure.

CAST. (*as before*). What do you think of that?

PABLO. I am not envious.

MAR. And the arms? Those who stamped their frenzied imaginings on embossments and indentations —what did they do?

LUC. The Infantes of Aragon—what did they do?

MAR. Come, it is all really admirable. There is a brick which comes, Don Castulo says, from Ecbatana, and which shows a slight depression, as it the end of a finger had sunk into the soft clay. And do you know what it was? Well, I at once made up a history; a poor slave was moulding it, and the overseer, or whatever he was called in those times, observing him walk lazily, struck him across the naked shoulders with the thong. I seem to be looking at it (*emphatically*), a lash of elephant hide with spikes of copper; is it not true, Don Castulo? (CASTULO *smiles*) and the slave cowered with pain and buried his finger in the clay. An eternal impress of human suffering on a morsel of pott   ; a petrified sorrow, which at the close of thousands of years tells us : " There have always been victims who writhe, executioners who scourge, and clay to preserve through centuries of centuries every cruelty."

CAST. Very good, very good.

TRIN. What a head !

CLARA. What imagination !

PABLO. She is very clever. (*To* DON JOAQUIN.)

JOAQ. Too clever.

LUC. (*aside to* CLARA). And in what clay will your cruelties be petrified ?

CLARA. Ask that of Castulo.

MAR. What irritates me is the impassiveness with which all those curiosities see us come and go. I should like them to become animated, to take part in our life : I should like the tears of yesterday to mingle with those of to-day, the passions of those people and our own passions to rush together in conflict.

CLARA. How fearful !

PABLO. But you never get into a passion.

JOAQ. You think not?

TRIN. Mariana never flies into a passion :—no, señor.

MAR. Well, I should fly into a passion. Let one of those objects take part in my existence, let it cause me one grief, and you should see how all those fragments of crockery would come rattling on to the floor.

CAST. Not quite so, Mariana.

LUC. Ah, if Mariana would do that !

JOAQ. Luciano is now growing indignant.

CAST. But none of you have seen the most curious thing of all.

MAR. The Mexican Saloon ?

CAST. That of course ; but there is something else ; a surprise which I reserve for Luciano.

LUC. Ah, my God !

TRIN. What is it?

JOAQ. What do you refer to?

PABLO. Have you not heard that it is for Luciano ?

CAST. For the present let us visit the Mexican Hall.

TRIN. Let us go there.

MAR. Daniel has not come.

CAST. We shall wait a while.

MAR. Yes; let us wait till Daniel comes. Ah ! he is very well versed in these matters. And you, Don Pablo?

PABLO. I am not, señora.

MAR. Well, he certainly is. According to what he has told me, so was his father—Señor de Montoya who has inestimable collections. Do you know of them, Don Castulo? Do you know Señor de Montoya ?

CAST. I have not the honour of his acquaintance. He always lives retired in his country seat.

MAR. Yes ; he is a great invalid.

CAST. I have heard that, away in Seville, he has many curiosities. But though he be an American and I belong to the Peninsula, I wager that my Mexican saloon is superior to his, if he really has one. I ? I have a storehouse of wonders. I have, above all, one object . . beneath a little lighthouse—which I would not part with for thirty thousand dollars. You (*To* MARIANA.) who have so much imagination, what histories you will invent when you see it !

MAR. (*with much interest*). What is it?

TRIN. Tell us, Don Castulo.

JOAQ. Prepare us.

PABLO. Indeed these things require preparation. Strong emotions cannot come all in a moment.

LUC. Well, they are coming.

MAR. Let us know . . let us know, Don Castulo. Take note that I am dying of curiosity.

CAST. The thing in question is what I call the Mexican pendant, which you will see described in all treatises on Archæology. It is a ring of gold from which there hang, by means of three little chains of the same metal, three small winged figures of elongated form and of perfect design, also of gold, and with the right hand upon the mouth. Eh! (*He says all this with emphasis, and rejoicing in the effect which he is producing. The ladies are seated; the gentlemen as may be most convenient to lend movement to the tableau.*)

TRIN. Come, then—like a lady's ear-ring.

CAST. Something like it, but not altogether so. Two of these pendants were found, as all the treatises declare, in a sepulchre which was discovered, thanks to certain exploratory diggings, in Tehuantepec. Two mummies were unearthed, undoubtedly of the race of Zapoteca, and each one had, fastened to the lower lip by its corresponding hook, one of these pendants. For each mummy, and for each lip of each mummy, there was its respective pendant. As one might say, to each its pendant. Eh?

MAR. What a curious thing! And what was it for?

CAST. It was an ornament which they wore in life. There are instances.

JOAQ. Then it could not have been an ornament for orators or women—though strictly speaking it should have been. (*All laugh.*)

CAST. Was it a sepulchral and symbolical object? It is not impossible. I say that they symbolise the eternal silence of those mummified lips.

TRIN. Ugh! what a horror!

MAR. Continue, Don Castulo.

CAST. Were they tokens of love from those two beings who throughout an eternity were sending each other frozen kisses by the little winged figures, messengers, among the shadows of death, of the caresses of life? Away, now, and verify it.

MAR. Yes; what doubt can there be? They are tokens of love . . . of eternal love.

PABLO. What an interest you take in winged figures, Mariana!

TRIN. Let's go and see them.

MAR. I shall not look at the Mexican pendant till Daniel comes. And how did you come into possession of that marvel? for you have said that it is a very rare object.

CAST. (*in a tone of vanity*). What? There is only one other like it in the world. Look in all the treatises. There are two of these pendants. I have one: the other is retained by the man who let me have mine. He let me have it in exchange for a Venus of the Classical period. But I gained by the exchange. Nobody gets the better of me. Sometimes I . . . manage that with others. (*Laughing.*)

PABLO. And who was the victim? Say—if you remember.

CAST. Fourteen or sixteen years have passed away; but I never forget the names of my victims. I knew him in Paris: he was a good fellow: a man of the world: of complicated history: in appearance very rich: he was very conspicuous in the Spanish-American republics: he afterwards disappeared, and I don't know what can have become of him. He must have died; because with the life that he led one does not live long.

PABLO. And he was named——?

CAST. Don Felix Alvarado.

MAR. (*rising, and unable to control herself*). Alvarado ! Alvarado !

JOAQ. (*aside*). For God's sake, Mariana !

CAST. Did you know him ?

MAR. I ? . . . How could that be ? Don Castulo, I am not yet a piece of antiquity. (*With a forced laugh.*)

CLARA (*to her husband*). What things you say !

MAR. At that time I was quite a child. Even had I known him I should not have remembered him. I was about to say—" Alvarado . . . Alvarado—the victim of Don Castulo !" Poor señor ! . . . A victim ! . . . Clarita, your husband is much to be feared. . . . But you see, Trinidad ! . . . Ah, Don Pablo, how implacable . . . at times . . . are the best of men ! . . . Why, do you not see what Don Castulo has done ? Poor Alvarado ! . . .

LUC. And he was left with the other pendant ?

CAST. That's evident.

JOAQ. But are we not going to see the Mexican saloon ?

MAR. Yes, go, you others, to see that curiosity. . . .

TRIN. Well, let us go.

LUC. Ha ! . . . we must all be there. . . .

CAST. (*embracing* LUCIANO *and laughing*). The archæological blood.

CLARA (*on seeing that all make a movement to go out and that* MARIANA *remains seated*). Aren't you coming ?

MAR. I have seen so many things in those galleries, and they have excited my nerves in such a way, that before receiving new impressions I should like to take a rest.

PABLO. Do you decidedly wish to wait for Daniel?

MAR. He understands a great deal about antiquities, and I should be glad to know what effect is produced on him by that pendant of sepulchral silence (*Laughing*), and how he interprets the tiny figures with the wings.

PABLO. I respect your wishes now, as always.

MAR. (*extending her hand to him*). You are very kind, Don Pablo. I respect you as a good gentleman and I esteem you as a loyal friend.

PABLO. Thanks, Mariana. (*To the others.*) Shall we go?

CAST. March!

CLARA (*with a caressing gesture to* MARIANA). Meditate, meditate and dream, capricious little head.

TRIN. Let us see how you will interlace that dead world (*Pointing to the galleries*) with this living world.

MAR. Everything is interlaced in this world, and I should not be astonished if the mummies of Tehuantepec arose from their couch to come and disturb my existence. (*Laughing.*)

TRIN. (*turning away from her*). What a Mariana it is!

JOAQ. (*contemplating her for a moment*). What a Mariana it is!

CAST. Walk on, walk on. . . .

PABLO. Let us now look upon prehistoric America.

LUC. Let us look upon it for the fifth time.

[*Exeunt all but* MARIANA.

MAR. Alvarado! . : . The wretch! . The man of the orgies in London! . He who killed my mother with shame and grief and hunger. For me to hear his name, and for all the dregs of hatred to roll together within my breast is one and the same thing.

No : there are some remembrances that do not pass
away with time. . . . Oh ! if Alvarado were alive !
If I could give him back sorrow for sorrow, shame
for shame, torture for torture ! Avenge my mother
on him and on his race ! (*A pause.*) Don Joaquin
is right : the impurities and miseries of my childhood
have left within me the germ of evil. Alvarado.
Alvarado   (*Enter* DANIEL.) Alvarado ! Ha !
(*Recovering herself.*) It is Daniel. (*In a tone o
sweetness.*)

DAN. Mariana ! . . .

MAR. (*giving him her hand*). It is you ! . . . I
thought   What madness ! . . . that it was some
one else.

DAN. Who?

MAR. How do I know? Some one else. There
are so many people in the world.

DAN. And who may that other be who has the
power to frighten my Mariana ?

MAR. Why, any one at all. I am so nervous to-
day that any one might have terrified me by entering
suddenly.

DAN. Even I ?

MAR. (*tenderly*). No ; not you. You are the only
one whom I look upon this day with pleasure.

DAN. Is it really so, Mariana ?

MAR. I was expecting you with such impatience !

DAN. You were expecting me?

MAR. Yes ; they wanted to take me with them to
go through the chamber of American antiquities ;
and I said : " No—not without Daniel ! " (*Caressingly.*) Come, doesn't that please you ?

DAN. But is it true? Did you mean it ?

MAR. I should think so : and not only did I mean
it ; I said: "I have the courage of my convictions

and of my affections." And when I like anybody, I proclaim it in a loud voice. And so I said: "I shall not see the chamber until Daniel comes: we shall see it together."

DAN. And did Don Pablo hear it?

MAR. Why not? They all heard it. And I said it in order that he might hear it. And now, complain and be jealous and say that I am bad. I may be very bad; but little by little I shall go on learning to love and to be good.

DAN. Good! My God, but you are an angel! I don't know what's passing over me, Mariana: I never have heard you say things like these.

MAR. Well, señor: don't be saying in a joke: angel. I am not one yet, but I feel within me that I am going to turn good. I still have from time to time my outbursts of anger and my moments of distrust. Even now . . . not long since . . . just before your arrival, I felt something very bad rolling to and fro in my heart—like a large, black figure of an angel that is broken by mischance. But you appeared, and I grew calm: in sober truth I grew calm. It cannot but be that you exercise over me a beneficent influence. You form around me an atmosphere, as it were, of peace, of confidence, of sweetness . . . of what else?

DAN. Say of affection—profound, immeasurable, eternal.

MAR. Well, here I say it—although we are making ourselves ridiculous—yes, I'll say it: of affection—profound, unalterable . . . what else was it?

DAN. Immeasurable and eternal.

MAR. Immeasurable and eternal. There you have it, Daniel.

DAN. Ah, my God, how happy a day this is for

me! Indeed I had a presentiment of it. On my
leaving home—a splendid sun, a glorious day. I
proposed to walk very fast, and a little girl barred my
path begging an alms from me "Get away, get
away!" I said. And then I remembered: "No, the
first time I saw Mariana she was giving alms to a
child."—"Come," I called to her: and there sprang
forward a cloud of children, and I gave them all the
money I had about me. What blessings! Well, I
have gathered up those blessings already in the form
of sweet utterances from my Mariana. If you love
me, I shall become a saint.

MAR. Poor Daniel!

DAN. I am not poor now. I am immensely rich
with hopes.

MAR. Mark me: no one has loved me in this
world with all fulness of soul except my mother, and
I have never sincerely loved any one but her. Well,
it seems to me that you likewise love me from your
heart. And it is plain that I too have a heart. I was
alone in the world with my rebellions, and my dis-
dains, and my doubts, and with no deep affection. I
became acquainted with you ; and what a battle there
was within me ! "He is like all the rest.—He is not
like all the rest." "He is hypocritical and selfish.—
He is not." "It is not love ; it is caprice.—It is not
caprice : it cannot be." And I go on convincing
myself that you are not like others, and that you are
not deceiving poor Mariana. (*In an imploring tone.*)
Do not deceive me, Daniel, in saying that you love
me so much !

DAN. I deceive you! Ask me for my life,
Mariana.

MAR. That is a trap. To ask of you your life for
ever is as much as to say : "Let us be married."

DAN. And even so?

MAR. We must go more gently. I am still rather diffident and very untractable.

DAN. How sweet your accent is, Mariana. After all, after all, you are my Mariana. Say yes.

MAR. Let us go by that pathway : let the rising ground come to the end of its ascent.

DAN. I am on the height calling to you, and you are very little short of it.

MAR. But that very little is very fatiguing.

DAN. Then I shall stretch out a hand to you.

MAR. This day you shall have no reason to complain of me. Neither shall you be sad.

DAN. This is the happiest day of my life.

MAR. (*turns to see if the others are coming*). It shall be so for us both.

DAN. Have no fear : they are not coming. They are surveying the old things.

MAR. And if they should come, what does it matter to me? I am free. Above all, I am free to say to them in a very loud voice · " My friends, I have lost my liberty." (*With a certain coquettish fondness.*)

DAN. When will you have that transport of courage and that transport of pity?

MAR. When? How can I tell ! Soon. If it should come upon me—this very moment. I am capable of saying to them : " Ladies and gentlemen, we have come to celebrate the inauguration of the Mexican Gallery; well, solemnity for solemnity. I announce to you that next month I inaugurate my new life, and invite you to my wedding." In those very words.

DAN. Don't make a farce of this. If it should not be possible ! (*Between fear and hope.*)

MAR. Not be possible !—Say that it is not regular :
but I love what's irregular, unforeseen, eccentric.

DAN. And why should it be irregular?

MAR. Even if it should be so   But, speaking
seriously, it is too soon.

DAN. How sad to hear that !

MAR. (*with much fondness*). Don't be sad. See,
now, this day I feel weak and compassionate
and if I see you in that condition, I shall begin when
you least expect it : " Ladies and gentlemen, we have
come to celebrate the inauguration . . ." (*Bursting
into laughter.*) What folly ! or what an announce-
ment of what's going to happen within a little while !
(*Continues to laugh.*)

DAN. Mariana, what power you have over me !
With a single sentence I am in heaven ; with another
sentence—in the bottomless abyss. And I don't
know where I am.

MAR. Let's have discretion. I don't know if it will
be to-day or to-morrow   but I shall either have
you for companion in this life, or I shall march alone
to the end. I shall be Daniel's or nobody's.

DAN. Then mine.

MAR. Why not ?

DAN. Then say it.

MAR. Ah, my God, how conquerors abuse their
victory !

DAN. Mariana !

MAR. Silence !

Re-enter, speaking with great animation, CLARA,
TRINIDAD, DON PABLO, DON CASTULO, LU-
CIANO, *and* DON JOAQUIN : *they enter at inter-
vals and form divers groups.*

JOAQ. Very curious . . . very curious,

PABLO. I am not intellectual, but I recognise that there are objects of much merit here.

CAST. Of merit ! Let Luciano tell you that.

LUC. In this house there are things of great price.

CAST. (*referring to* LUCIANO). He is the one who should know it.

TRIN. Well, what I have been most pleased with is what Don Castulo said.

CLARA. Now that Daniel is here (*To* MARIANA.) you should go and see it. It's most beautiful.

TRIN. Yes, Mariana : you will like it very much.

JOAQ. Go with her, Daniel.

DAN. I am at her orders.

MAR. (*to* DANIEL). Will you come? Then let us go there. But you come, Don Castulo.

CAST. Most assuredly. You'll see, you'll see, Daniel. You are intelligent, but you know nothing to equal it.

DAN. And what is it?

MAR. A most curious thing, Daniel. (*With much amiability, and even in a familiar tone.*)

CAST. I have already explained it just now. A ring of gold with three pendants : each one is composed of a small chain—also of gold—and of a little figure with wings. . . .

DAN. (*laughing*). Yes, I know already: and with the hand upon the mouth : one cannot know whether it sends a kiss or is imposing silence.

CAST. That's it : ah ! you know . . . ?

DAN. (*in a triumphant tone*). Why, what have you imagined? It is what you call among yourselves, " The two Mexican pendants—unique in the archæological world !"

MAR. And so you know them? What this Daniel

does know ! Don Castulo, would you have imagined it ?

CAST. (*sadly and humbly*). It is true : there are two ; but I have no more than one.

DAN. (*laughing*). I can well believe it.

CAST. So that you have seen them ?

DAN. Many times.

CAST. (*disdainfully*). Sketches—in books : a kind of fac-simile.

DAN. No—the other one : the fellow of that which you have.

MAR. How ? . . . You ? . . . In what way ? (*In surprise.*)

CAST. (*disdainfully*). Good : you will have seen it, but you do not possess it.

DAN. (*in a tone of jesting, of triumph, of great merriment*). So . . . so ! . . . Do you not hear, Mariana ? What vanity these learned men are filled with ! He believed it was the only one.

MAR. I don't understand . . (*To* DANIEL.) You say. . . . Go on. . . . (*All the rest of this scene is commended to the intelligence of the actress.*)

TRIN. Let us know, let us know—how is that ?

LUC. Everything is becoming a curiosity in this house—isn't it a fact, Don Pablo ?

PABLO. So I believe.

MAR. Very curious. Eh, Don Joaquin ?

JOAQ. We are about to see.

DAN. There is nothing to wonder at ; if that object is what you suppose it to be, and not a counterfeit. . . .

CAST. How a counterfeit !

MAR. Perhaps it is.

CAST. Gently, gently : it is not. I have a legal record : seven witnesses : certified by the consul at

Tehuantepec—and the consul of Tehuantepec isn't a nobody. Ho, ho, there! Counterfeit! What do you say to that, Luciano?

Luc. That I am half dead with horror, Don Castulo.

Cast. Counterfeit!

Dan. Don't be alarmed : the pendant must be legitimate. But if it be so, the fellow of it is almost mine; because it was my father who superintended the excavations, and from that time onward it has been in his museum.

Mar. Daniel! . . . Daniel! . . . No! . . . No! . . . It is not true !

Joaq. (controlling her). For God's sake ! . . .

Dan. But, Mariana, what interest do you take in a thing . . . that makes me laugh?

Mar. And me also. (Laughing nervously.) You don't know, Daniel. . . . But it is really impossible. It is impossible. . . . Ha, ha, ha ! . . . How horrible it would be, Don Joaquin ! (Clinging to him.)

Cast. But I repeat that the man who conceded to me that spoil of the tomb of Tehuantepec was an American.

Dan. It might be—no ; it was my father.

Cast. No ; it was not Señor de Montoya.

Mar. (violently). Don't be obstinate, Daniel; it was not Montoya. What a man you are ! . . . No Daniel. . . . (Coming close to him, and speaking tenderly.) It was not your father ! . . Speak the truth—it was not—eh?

Dan. Why not?

Cast. Because the American was named Don Felix Alvarado.

Dan. And what difficulty is there in that? My

father in his political adventures . . . in his secret
missions . . . in his travels to Europe . . . many
times . . .

MAR. Changed his name?

DAN. Exactly: the conspirator's precautions. . .
In America he was called Don Enrique Montoya: in
Spain, Don Felix Alvarado.

MAR. So that now there is no hope?

DAN. Hope! Of what?

MAR. Of Don Castulo making up his pair of
curiosities: your father will not care to deprive
himself of so inestimable an object.

DAN. On the contrary, now that you are so much
interested in these objects, that I may afford a
pleasure to Don Castulo, and that you may see the
two pendants together, our good friend may, from this
day, count upon having the companion pendant. Are
you both satisfied?

CAST. Montoya! Montoya! . . . You are a man
of heart! (*Embraces* DANIEL, *who laughs
merrily.*) This day I will invite you all to another
breakfast to celebrate the definitive union of the two
Mexican pendants. In the depth of a tomb they
were united by death: Montoya separated them: I
am about to reunite them.

MAR. How poetical, Don Castulo! Poetry is
infectious. And I am thinking . . . Shall I say it?

JOAQ (*aside*). Mariana, what are you about to
do?

MAR. (*aside*). To raise a barrier this very moment
between that man and me.

JOAQ. (*aside*). Why?

MAR. (*aside*). Because I love him. I am so infamous that I still love him. (*Aloud.*) And so I am
going to declare it. On that solemn day we shall

celebrate another definitive union. . . . There will be another pair. . . . What a life it is, Daniel!

TRIN. Another union?

CLARA. Which one?

MAR. It is a secret. (*Aside to* PABLO.) Don Pablo, I accept your offer.

PABLO (*aside to her*). My wife?

MAR. (*aside*). Yes.

PABLO (*aside*). You render me the happiest of men. (*Kisses her hand.*)

CLARA. But what about us?

LUC. It cannot be: no secrets can be admitted here to-day.

DAN. That would be a cruelty. For God's sake, Mariana, by that which you love most or have loved most in this world. . . . I entreat you.

MAR. The one whom I loved most was my mother.

DAN. Then by the memory of your mother.

MAR. (*after a pause*). Then   by her memory .. I announce to you, my good friends, that I intend to be the wife of Don Pablo Arteaga.

DAN. What? What does she say? She! Mariana his wife?

MAR. Yes,—his wife.

DAN. It is not true, Mariana. And if it be true, it is an infamy.

PABLO. Señor de Montoya, that insult I pluck away from Mariana; I take it to myself, and I shall inflict chastisement for it.

DAN. Señor de Arteaga, upon you I'll bring down the chastisement due to both—for her treachery and your scorn. I swear it by the name of my father.

MAR. Which father? Montoya or Alvarado?

DAN. Montoya!

PABLO. Enough!

MAR. (*aside*). Ah! . . . My Daniel!

DAN. Ah! wretches—there is no worldly consideration that shall withhold me.

JOAQ. For God's sake!

CLARA. Daniel!

CAST. Have sense, . . .

LUC. Be prudent, . . .

TRIN. This is too much.

MAR. (*aside*). Mother, my own mother, I could not have done more for you.

DAN. (*as the actors are arranged in a final group*). Ah! She . . . she! Yes! I see it clear as light . . . she has played with my heart. She has tortured my soul. She has maddened my brain. . . . Miserable woman! . . . (*To* DON PABLO). And wretch that you are! . . . Wretch that I am myself! . . . Pass on—out of my sight . . . or I shall not be answerable for what I do. . . . Mariana, Mariana, you shall remember me! Yes. . . . You shall remember, . . . Oh! that woman and that man! . . . How they'll have reason to remember Daniel Montoya!

END OF ACT III.

EPILOGUE.

PERSONAGES :

MARIANA.
DANIEL.
DON PABLO.
DON JOAQUIN.
DON CASTULO.
LUCIANO.
FELIPE, *a male servant from Galicia.*
CLAUDIA, *a female servant from Andalusia.*

The scene is in a country seat belonging to MARIANA, *in La Granja, or near it.*

The stage represents a drawing-room on the ground floor of a country seat of MARIANA *in La Granja. In the back-centre a large door looking on to a terrace: on either side of the door are great windows with transparent panes of glass. Beyond these are visible the terrace, its flowers, and the trees in the garden. At the first wing, to right and left, are two little doors which lead to two private rooms. In the second wing there are two other and larger doors—that on the left of the spectator being supposed to lead to the suite of apartments of* MARIANA, *the corresponding one*

to the right leading to the apartments of DON
PABLO. *The drawing-room is adorned with great
luxuriance and elegance. It is night : candelabra
are upon the tables : the sky is blue and clear :
the moon shines at opportune moments, inundating
with its clear radiance all the background; at
other times the light becomes obscure, as though
concealed by some cloud.*

Enter CLAUDIA *and* FELIPE. *They go about the
room, arranging it, fixing flowers, &c.*

FELIPE. Is everything in order ?

CLAUDIA. Everything.

FEL. The bride and bridegroom will soon be here,
and the bridegroom must have everything in perfect
readiness. It is a fact.

CLAUD. Well, let them come. But they won't be
bride and bridegroom now : they'll be husband and
wife.

FEL. I say that they'll be bride and bridegroom.

CLAUD. They would have been married in Madrid
at eight o'clock : they will have afterwards taken the
special train which Doña Mariana ordered to be at
her disposal, and from there they must have come on
at full speed : it is half-past eleven or twelve, so that
they bear the weight of three hours of marriage.

FEL. Three hours longer of the part of bride and
bridegroom ; it is a fact.

CLAUD. How pig-headed you are !

FEL. I am a reflecting man, that's what I am : it's
a fact.

CLAUD. You are a dull man—that's what you are :
it's a fact. (*Mocking him.*)

FEL. Have you put flowers in the señora's room?

CLAUD. I have put them there, and made a garden

of it. And also in the señor's room, **and** it is turned into another garden.

FEL. Flowers in the senor's room! Now, do you see how thoughtless you are?

CLAUD. In what way?

FEL. What, my dear girl? Bits of flowers for a soldier like Don Pablo, who, as they say, is more warlike than Sant Iago! With more scars and more glittering decorations, and who must have killed more people! . . .

CLAUD. Kill! kill! Many people kill—with the result that no one dies. He may kill . . .; but before the marriage he fought a duel—do you hear? And he was pinked! He was pinked by Don Daniel, who is a fine fellow . . . he is the one to pink and slay, with those great Malaga eyes of his. I know him—do you understand? Well, he pinked Don Pablo.

FEL. Indeed?

CLAUD. As I tell you: I heard it in Madrid.

FEL. My dear girl, such are the events of life. He who places himself before the point of a sword must be pinked—if God brings no remedy. It's a fact. And what was it about?

CLAUD. I don't know: Don Pablo and Don Daniel were having hot words together, and as they are both fierce fellows. . . . You now understand. But Don Daniel is the fiercer of the two.

FEL. It must have been about our young lady.

CLAUD. It may be, for she is so pretty—so wonderfully pretty! What are men good for except to kill one another for sake of the pretty girls?

FEL. And how rich she is!—so rich! What are men good for except to have an eye on the morrow? It's a fact.

CLAUD. That you may say for the husband. As for Daniel, neither in attitude of body, nor in possession of property, nor in loving with all his soul, nor in worth of heart, need he be envious of any man.—What are you laughing at, stupid?

FEL. Because I know more about all this than you: I know how they quarrelled, and why, and what was the result.

CLAUD. And why did you act the know-nothing, slyboots?

FEL. To see if you knew anything fresh. But I know more than you.

CLAUD. Well, out with it.

FEL. There was a duel; but Don Daniel did not pink him—that's *not* a fact.

CLAUD. Yes, yes. It's true.

FEL. No! Don Daniel, as he is younger, and as he was in a rage, with one stroke after another, disarmed Don Pablo three times—it's a fact.

CLAUD. Have you seen him? Do you know Don Daniel?

FEL. By name—nothing more. With my eyes I have never seen him.

CLAUD. And what else? Go on.

FEL. Don Pablo, too, was in a rage. When such an accident befalls a man he's bound to be in a rage. And he said, "Younger than I am, and with stronger arms!" It seems that Don Daniel has great muscle.

CLAUD. Very great. And what then?

FEL. That the young one said, "Well, let us try shooting." And they tried shooting. And Don Pablo had a better aim than Don Daniel, and planted a ball in his breast. The young one is more muscular: it's a fact. But the old fellow aimed better: it's a fact.

CLAUD. And Don Daniel is dead? Ah, poor fellow!

FEL. When you say dying—he did not die. But he was very bad—very bad, and he is still in bed suffering greatly.

CLAUD. But he has escaped with life?

FEL. He has escaped, woman; he has escaped.

CLAUD. And Don Pablo?—Don Pablo . . . got away with nothing?

FEL. No: he, too, had his little crumb of a bullet. Only it struck against a rib and bounded off: old men's bones are very hard: it's a fact.

CLAUD. So then he is an old piece of goods?

FEL. No, he is not a cripple :—well preserved, erect, robust, and brave. But come, he is not in his first youth.

CLAUD. What will he be?

FEL. I don't know what he will be :—it's a fact.

CLAUD. I speak of his years.

FEL. Oh! somewhere about fifty.

CLAUD. Ave Maria Purissima! And the señorita deserts Don Daniel and gets married to that stalking statue! A fine taste the ladies of the present day have! Bah!—I must deprive Don Pablo of his flowers: flowers for him! I shall have to send to the druggist's for barley-water and put it in his room, with a basin of broth, a glass of sherry, and a foot-warmer.

FEL. He will have brought a footwarmer with him : because, as you know, when travelling . . . it's a fact.

CLAUD. I am dying to see him : does he throw his money about?

FEL. I don't know if he scatters money about, for although I asked that from the servants who arrived this morning from Madrid—and it was from them I got the news I have given you—they did not tell me. But as for knowing him, you'll soon know him, because the carriages went some time ago to the station to fetch them all, and they cannot be long.

CLAUD. Do you mean that a great many people are coming?

FEL. Some people are coming, but not many are coming.

CLAUD. And are they all to sleep here? Ah, my God, when nothing has been said to me!

FEL. Don't be frightened, for as to sleeping, none but the bride and bridegroom will sleep. As the others are not brides and bridegrooms, Don Joaquin will take them all away to his country seat.

CLAUD. I know, I know already: he built it hereabouts to have Doña Mariana within view.

FEL. The very same. And talking about viewing. Look, I think they are here already. Don't you hear a noise of carriages?

CLAUD. Yes. (*Goes to the door of the private room to the left.*)

FEL. Where are you going?

CLAUD. To look through the window of the study and see if the carriages are coming.

FEL. You can't go in.

CLAUD. I can't go in to the señora's little private room?

FEL. No, señora.

CLAUD. Why, you drone?

FEL. Because the key has been lost.

CLAUD. It has been lost?

FEL. Some one has taken it away.

CLAUD. Who?

FEL. The devil—the same who takes away all keys.

CLAUD. What are you talking about?

FEL. This evening there came a gentleman—a young man ; he was young and of good appearance. He said he belonged to the press—to those people who see everything so as to relate everything in the newspapers : it's a fact. As our señora's wedding was so much talked about, and the palace is so lovely. .

CLAUD. He wished to see it?

FEL. And he saw it—I should think so: and everything that he saw will be put down in the newspapers: there's an honour for the señora and for all of us. But

CLAUD. What?

FEL. On leaving that private room — through absence of mind—I say it must have been through absence of mind—he took away the key.

CLAUD. But—gracious ! . . . And if the señora wishes to enter?

FEL. I can get through the window, which is on a level with the ground, and open the door.

CLAUD. You will really have to do something.

FEL. Silence ! . . . They are knocking for attendance, and now you have them here.

Enter DON CASTULO *and* LUCIANO *by the back-centre.*

SERVANT (*preceding them*). Walk in.

FEL. Walk in, señores ; walk in.

LUC. This must be a handsome property.

CAST. They say so: it has a reputation. Great luxury ! Modern industry: modern art : everything modern ; but it has a reputation, in spite of being modern.

FEL. Pardon me, señores : . . . are not the other señores coming?

LUC. They will be here within five minutes.

FEL. Well if you, señores, do not require anything, we shall go and wait for the other señores—with year permission.

LUC. You may go. [*Exeunt* CLAUDIA *and* FELIPE.

CAST. (*looking at everything in leisurely fashion*). Nothing : just what I told you. Great splendour, much ostentation. A veritable palace : almost a royal palace. But not an object that's worth the trouble of men like ourselves fixing our attention upon. (*Contemptuously.*) Modernism : pure modernism. There is nothing here stamped by the seal of individuality : there is nothing here which can be, say, sixty years old, say fifty.

LUC. Well, you are already fifty : and you are here.

CAST. Don't speak to me of persons : neither do they go beyond a hundred years. In the class of persons, the only ones acceptable are mummies. [1] " Pick up the most despicable object, throw it back to a distance of two thousand years, and it becomes changed into an object of incomparable value by the work and favour of that marvellous artificer who is called *time*. I laugh at *Apollo* when he is compared with *Saturn*. Put in a bottle a fool of our own days : preserve him for six thousand years, and see if, when he is unbottled at the proper time in the coming ages, the wisest man of the seventy-ninth century can compare with him.

LUC. Don Castulo, you have a profundity which fills one with terror.

CAST. (*modestly*). I am a man with a partiality for universal life."

---

[1] AUTHOR'S NOTE.—In order to lighten this scene in the representation, whatever is within inverted commas may be omitted.

LUC. (*looking toward the background*). But are they not coming?

CAST. I think not : but they'll soon come.

LUC. One of the horses of the other carriage cast his shoe, and it appears that the loss of it must have been rather painful to him still. That must have been the cause of the delay.

CAST. (*giving him a slap on the back and laughing*). Now . . . now I understand you.

LUC. Me?

CAST. You are getting over me in a roundabout way.

LUC. I . . . you, Don Castulo ! . . . Do you believe

CAST. That's your way of putting it. Since I intimated to you that I had in reserve for you a certain surprise, you have not known how to live. All your ways have been indirect, circumlocutory, artful ; I understand you.

LUC. I assure you . . .

CAST. Don't assure me of anything. " You know, assuredly, all the precious relics of my house : all its secrets and corners. . . .

LUC. (*modestly*). Not all.

CAST. Not all—there I believe you. There is something which you have not yet seen, and which I have reserved as a reward of your constancy and your love of archæology. What do you think of that?

LUC. I don't understand you.

CAST. You understand me. If not, why do I find you at all hours in my house? Eh? Don't blush, don't be uneasy : your partialities delight me—for they are the same as my own.

LUC. So I think.

CAST. Very well, then : learn it and give a place in

your breast to hope. As soon as we have ended this
expedition and have returned to Madrid I shall withdraw from before your astonished gaze the last veil
over my august habitation : shall we call it august?

LUC. Call it what you please, but draw it aside.

CAST. Oh ! how natural is such impatience." What
a collection, friend Luciano ! The most humble, the
most prosaic, and, in the profoundest sense, the most
sublime ! I would not say this except to one who,
like yourself, could understand me : from the Egyptian
until our own days . . . a complete collection of *horseshoes !* What do you think of that ?

LUC. The devil ! Horseshoes !

CAST. Horseshoes. The iron hoof-protectors of
that generous brute which is called the horse. *Equus*
in Latin : 'Ιππος in Greek ! . Yes, you had guessed
it : you are worthy indeed of having guessed it.

LUC. Many thanks.

CAST. You do well, Luciano : you do well to interest
yourself in the archæology of so modest a type. "No
one will tax me with vanity when I say that I have
horseshoes from as far back as those of *Pegasus* down
to those of *Rocinante;* from the Pharaonic, Persian, and
Tartarean horseshoes down to those of the Cossack
cavalry ; from the horseshoes of Attila, that annihi-
lated all grass, down to the horseshoes of Napoleon,
which, as the seal of revolutionary conquest, move
along stamping with blood all the continents. When
I say the horseshoes of Attila and Napoleon, I mean
those of their respective hippogriffs.

LUC. That's understood."

CAST. All civilisations and all horseshoes have
constantly clashed together along the path of history.
You have an example of this now. Thus, my cabinet
of horseshoes—what else is it but a collection of

irons and of tortuous annals?   What horseshoes,
friend Luciano.   I shall put them to you. . . .

LUC. Good God, Don Castulo !

CAST. Let me finish.   I shall put them before you,
and you shall read fluently, as you might read in the
pages of Tacitus, Titus Livius, or Cesare Cantu.[1]
It is, indeed, appalling, Luciano.   It is, indeed, appalling.   Catch an Arab horse, throw his four hoofs
in the air, and you have all the Arabic architecture:
the arch of the horseshoe.   Without ironing all is
erring.   Without that marvellous and humble iron all
is error, and dulness, and confusion.

LUC. "And talking of errors (*Wishing to change the
conversation*), don't you think the recently-married
couple have committed a capital one in uniting
themselves with an indissoluble tie for the whole of
their lives?

CAST. I don't know.   I don't concern myself much
with those things.

LUC. Haven't you observed Mariana?   What
cadaverous paleness !   What a forced smile !   What
nervous excitement !

CAST. I have observed nothing.   My imagination
was hurrying onward in the footsteps of other imaginations.

LUC. On the termination of the ceremony there
came over her something like a fainting fit, and along
the whole way. . . . sepulchral silence !

CAST. Emotions appropriate to the wedding-day.
Look you, I too was rather moved when I was
married to Clarita.

LUC. I believe it.

CAST. Yes, señor.   So moved was I that day that

---

[1] The author of the "Storia Universale," &c.

I stupidly broke an Etruscan amphora. An irre-
parable loss, friend Luciano."

LUC. Well, I think they are now here.

CAST. No doubt they will be. To arrive at a place
there's nothing like proceeding towards it Sooner or
later you get there.

Enter MARIANA, DON PABLO *and* DON JOAQUIN
by the back-centre. MARIANA *pale and gloomy.
She walks with some difficulty, leaning on the
arm of* DON JOAQUIN, *and sinks upon a sofa or
cushioned chair after having taken off her hat.*

JOAQ. Sit down and rest. You are not well.

PABLO. How do you feel?

MAR. Well, very well. There's nothing the matter
with me. Good God, what a child I am!

JOAQ. You are very pale.

PABLO. Very pale.

MAR. So many people speak, . . . and the saluta-
tions, the good wishes, the social impertinences!
To have to answer everybody. The smiles, the
courteous phrases, the commonplaces, become ex-
hausted,   and the nerves can hold out no longer.
The commonplace, which is self-imposed, is that
which is most wearisome and most exciting. . . .
and nothing else ails me. (*Endeavouring to smile.*)

PABLO. So that you are better?

MAR. I should hope so. (*With ill controlled impatience.*) I really say that it is nothing.

JOAQ. Nevertheless, in coming from Madrid to La
Granja you were not well. Two or three times I
thought you were becoming insensible.

LUC. I, too, remarked that.

CAST. I did not.

MAR. The train rushed on with such dizzying

velocity that I felt . . . I don't know what, . . . and
I closed my eyes and allowed myself to be whirled
along.   Do we not enter the train voluntarily?   Well,
we must close our eyes and let ourselves be borne
helplessly away.   (*With a forced laugh.*)   Such is life.
(*To* PABLO.)   Don't be alarmed: I am very well.
And I am pleased to find myself in my home . . .
in our home   . free from prying people and from
friends.   Oh! I don't mean that for you (*To* DON
CASTULO and LUCIANO) . . . nor for you (To DON
JOAQUIN), my own father.

CAST. We, too, shall withdraw, that discretion may
not clash with friendship.

LUC. Nor with Archæology.

CAST. Archæology is discretion itself: it says
everything in the form of silence.

MAR. That's why I am fond of it.   Silence!
What eloquence there is in silence!   (*To* DON
PABLO.)   Is it not true?

PABLO. It is my only eloquence.

CAST. And so we shall withdraw.

LUC. We are expected at Don Joaquin's villa.

MAR. Not yet; for God's sake!   (*Attempting to
smile.*)   You have to see the house.   The common
people in their emphatic style call it " the palace."
It is not quite that.   But from the drawing-room
above, the view on a clear, moonlit night, such as we
have now, is delicious.   Go upstairs: for persons of
imagination, like yourselves, it will be an admirable
spectacle.

LUC. However, if we are giving trouble . . .

MAR. By no means : we'll say ten minutes.   I shall
detain you ten minutes—no more.   Pablo, do me the
favour to accompany them ; it is fitting that you
should do the honours . . . as lord of the manor

... meanwhile I shall rest. (*She says all this and goes through all the scene with ease, with propriety, with something of irony, and, above all, with profound melancholy. She is always the great lady who knows how to control herself and to pay the debt due to social requirements.*)

PABLO. Shall we go there?

CAST. We are at your orders.

MAR. (*To* DON JOAQUIN). You know the house: you remain.

JOAQ. As you please.

PABLO. I shall go on in front to show you the way.

LUC. It's all really enchanting.

CAST. It is not bad, it is not bad: but in five hundred years' time it will look better.

[*Exeunt, by the second wing to the right,* PABLO, CASTULO, *and* LUCIANO.]

JOAQ. What's the matter with you, Mariana?

MAR. The matter is that the whole universe is formed of lead, and is weighing down upon me. I can no more, Don Joaquin. I can no more, my own father.

JOAQ. Oh! temper of iron! You now repent (*approaching her, and speaking in a low voice*), when the time is gone for ever.

MAR. Repent! No. What I did was well done. Unless I wished to be the most miserable woman on earth, I could not have done otherwise. It was not madness: it was not giddiness; it was honourable oresight and just chastisement.

JOAQ. Ah! blind and headstrong woman!

MAR. No, Don Joaquin: it was not blindness, it was not stubbornness. I wished to raise a barrier between Daniel and myself; I wished to set at my side a man who shall subdue my madness with a hand of iron, an implacable man, who, when I find myself going towards Daniel . . . for I know myself: if he does not come to me, I shall go to him. . . . Well, then ; when that event takes place, that Don Pablo shall kill me and kill him :—and perhaps, to save my Daniel, I shall have the strength to withstand the impulses of my delirium.

JOAQ. You are not convincing me . . . but, in short, it is now done. . . .

MAR. I don't convince you! But can you not guess all that I thought, all that I suffered on that day? Insomuch, that I was saying to myself—the only man for whom I have ever felt love was the son of Alvarado! I in love with the son of that wretch who dishonoured, who martyred, who murdered my mother ! . . Then . . . what sort of a conscience is mine? What kind of a woman can I be? Of what infamous and degraded substance must I be formed ?

JOAQ. These are exaggerations : when you were in love with Daniel you were ignorant of all that.

MAR. But I learned it since, and I continued to love him : now I know it, and my heart goes out of me towards my own Daniel.

JOAQ. Silence ! . . . silence ! . . . Don't say such things. . . . No more, no more !

MAR. Is it not true that all this is monstrous? That accursed race has brought about the damnation of mine ! His father disgraced my mother: and Daniel disgraces me. . . . What infamy ! . . . what infamy ! . Jesus ! . . . Jesus !

JOAQ. My daughter, it is the commandment of God : the sins of the fathers are visited upon the children.

MAR. But if he is innocent—why must he pay for the infamies of his father ?

JOAQ. Don't make me mad. You should have thought of all this before, and been married to Daniel.

MAR. That—never. You are too pure and too noble to mean what you say. I his wife! I united for ever to the son of Alvarado! and the two of us on the day of the wedding to go and receive the blessing, and the kiss of that man! Those lips which defiled the mother, deposing themselves with a burlesque sanctification upon the brow of the daughter! and then, when Daniel would speak to me of his love—to be always thinking, always having it in my mind,—that, that was what his father said to turn the brain of that poor martyr!—with the same serious voice, the same tenderness, the same transports of passion! Thus, thus that man dishonoured my mother, the mother of my heart! The blood of Daniel, his smile, the light of his eyes, the burning warmth of his hands, his sweet words! . . . All comes from that source! The daughter wallowing in the dregs of those impurities! No, no, no—anything rather than that eternal and revolting infliction. The woman who while thinking all this yet loves—for she does love—the son of Alvarado—ought to be the wife of Don Pablo : for her impunity, the ice-cold curb; for her madness, the straight waistcoat; for the wild beast without a heart, the merciless tamer!

JOAQ. Then you have found what you were looking for. When Don Pablo had suspicions of his first wife . . .

MAR. What ?

JOAQ. Coldly, impassibly, implacably, without a cry, without a recrimination . . . . without a menace , . .

MAR. What, then?

JOAQ. There are those who say, or at least suspect, that he found means to kill her with a single blow.

MAR. And can he have forgotten it?

JOAQ. I think not.

MAR. Would to God

JOAQ. Silence : they are coming back. (*Going to the door.*)

MAR. Let us pretend to be speaking of indifferent matters.

Re-enter PABLO, CASTULO, *and* LUCIANO.

LUC. Admirable, Mariana : an enchanted palace.

MAR. Really?

CAST. There is something: yes, there is something. I speak of what I am familiar with. Those carpets are good. And those enamels . . . they are of value . . they are of value. . . . And that beaten silver . . we could steal it with a good will—could we not, Luciano?

LUC. I would not steal anything, Don Castulo.

CAST. Would you never rob me of anything? Come, . . . come. . . .

LUC. (*slowly*). Perhaps so.

CAST. I knew it already. (*Thrusting at him playfully.*)

PABLO (*to* MARIANA). How are you?

MAR. The sickness of the journey has not left me. I suspect that I am going to have a very violent megrim.

JOAQ. Then, child, you must have rest.

LUC. With your permission we shall retire. The coach is waiting for us, (*To* MARIANA.) and Don Joaquin's country house is waiting for us.

CAST. (*taking leave*). Mariana . . . I am your

sincere friend, and the happiness of my friends, male and female . . . though it is not an object which can be included in my museum—does nevertheless afford me a most singular pleasure.

MAR. A thousand thanks, Don Castulo. I preserve remembrances of your museum which will not easily be erased from my mind—believe me.

CAST. A thousand thanks, Mariana. Adieu, Don Pablo : I am your sincere friend, and the happiness of my friends, male and female . . . though it is not an object . . . (LUCIANO *places himself between the two and laughingly separates them.* DON PABLO *and* DON CASTULO *walk toward the terrace, murmuring exchanges of compliment.*)

LUC. Good ! . . . Good ! Adieu, Mariana ; I am always yours.

MAR. Adieu, Luciano. (*They shake hands.*)

JOAQ. Adieu . . . adieu, my daughter . . . (LUCIANO *joins* CASTULO *and* PABLO *on the terrace.*)

MAR. Farewell, my own father. (*She and* JOAQUIN *embrace.*)

JOAQ. Courage ! . . .

MAR. I have too much courage. . . . It is happiness that I am in want of.

JOAQ. Farewell !

MAR. Farewell ! . . . (*The four men bid each other good-bye upon the terrace, where they are seen for some moments*)—I shall go into my bedroom. (*Stopping.*) No: he would come in. Into my sitting-room. (*Goes to the door of the study, then changes her intention.*)— But why ? (*Looking whether they are going.*) I shall go to my bedroom and lock myself in. No : I shall remain. (*Sinks upon a sofa.*) They are going now. Now they have gone. He is coming back. What matter ?

PABLO (*returning*). Are you better?

MAR. No, I have a ring of iron around the forehead. Of iron made red-hot : it oppresses and burns. Is that pleasant?

PABLO (*softly*). Poor Mariana!

MAR. Have the others gone?

PABLO (*approaching close to* MARIANA). Yes.

MAR. (*as if in the effort to say something*). Come!— so they have gone.

PABLO (*sitting close to her*). And have left us alone.

MAR. Excuse me . . . will you shut that door? (*Pointing to the door in the back-centre.*)

PABLO. Most certainly. (*Shuts the door.*) The night air was troubling you?

MAR. When I am as now   everything troubles me.

PABLO. I, too?

MAR. What a question!

PABLO. Don't you wish that we should speak?

MAR. Yes : you may speak; but pardon me if my answers are brief.   Each word pronounced by me resounds in my brain like the blow of a hammer upon an empty case.

PABLO. You have said : "your answers."   Do you suppose that my words will take the form of questions?

MAR. I said it for the sake of speaking, and now you may suppose that if I am not in a condition to speak, I am still less able to enter into discussion.

PABLO. Then I too will refrain from speaking.

MAR. As you please : silence is the only thing which ceases my pain.

PABLO. Silence and *solitude*—is it not so? *Solitude* and silence.

MAR. They are good companions; but I did not mean quite so much.

PABLO (*taking her hand*). Poor Mariana: your hand is like ice.

MAR. Didn't I tell you so? I am not well. Let it go . . . let go. . . . Excuse me. . . . (*Pulling away her hand.*) I must try to get it warm again. (*Muffling up her hands and sinking further back upon the sofa as if to fly from* PABLO.)

PABLO (*on seeing that she closes her eyes and lets fall her head*). Are you sleepy?

MAR. A little. Do you know, I think that with sleep this trouble would pass away from me.

PABLO. Then sleep for a short time and see if it will refresh you. I'll watch over you from this couch.

MAR. No: sleeping for a short time will not be enough. I require a long sleep—very long. For great sorrow we must have sleep that lasts a great while.

PABLO. Poor Mariana! You women are very weak.

MAR. It's true; and I am weaker than others.

PABLO. That's why you, who may be so, require a husband who shall love you from his soul, but who shall guide you with a firm hand. For your sufferings are often pure fantasy. "I am ill: I am ill," you women say in a soft and plaintive voice, as you said just now; and if a voice, affectionate but energetic says to you: "You are not ill: you are not ill: I don't wish you to be ill . . ."——Miracle of affection! You are well at once. Isn't that so? (*He says all this as if jestingly, but it is visible that he controls himself with effort, and that in his manner there is an undertone of domineering hardness.*)

MAR. (*coldly*). No: it is not so. This night I feel

really ill. And even if you should say to me with all the fondness and all the energy imaginable : " Don't be ill : I will not have it so," I should continue to be ill —in spite of the command ! (*With an ironical smile.*)

PABLO. I do not command, Mariana : I entreat.

MAR. So I suppose, and I am glad of it. It is too soon to command. But, ah, my God ! you see, I have spoken a little. The pain has increased, and is now grown intolerable. (*Pressing her forehead.*)

PABLO (*on the point of bursting into a rage*). For all that . . .

MAR. (*with dignity and haughtiness*). What ?

PABLO. I don't insist :—we shall see whether with silence, rest, and sleep, your suffering will pass off.

MAR. Thank you.

PABLO. Do you wish me to accompany you to your bedroom ?

MAR. No : excuse me. I shall be well enough here : the first sleep . . . here.

PABLO (*after a pause, in which he silently contemplates her*). Adieu, Mariana : sleep, take rest . . . I am not a tyrant : you wish to be alone and I leave you.

MAR. I am obliged to you, Pablo. Adieu.

PABLO. Won't you give me your hand ?

MAR. Why not ? . . .

PABLO. It is burning now.

MAR. Indeed ? . . . . Let me see . . . (*Withdrawing her hand*). I think you are right.

PABLO. Good-bye till to-morrow. (*Turning towards his bedroom.*)

MAR. (*without looking at him*). Till to-morrow.

PABLO (*at the door of his room, but without entering. Aside*). She has a will of iron. All the better.

MAR. I believe he has gone at last. He leaves me alone. To-morrow we shall see. He thinks to subdue me; that's not so easy. (PABLO *still stops at the door of his room. From that position he contemplates* MARIANA. MARIANA *turns to see if he has gone. On noting her movement* PABLO *comes back.*)

PABLO (*in a hard and resolute tone*). Pardon me: one more word.

MAR. (*with an irritation which she does not attempt to conceal*). Again!

PABLO. Oh, it will be very brief. . . . I know that you have married me without loving me, but I don't know why you have married. I knew that you were honourable and that was enough for me. You don't love me to-day? It does not matter; love may impress itself upon others: mine will impress itself. I wished that you should be mine: so you at present are: there is now time to make the rest come true. This is the way with me: if I propose to myself to succeed in a thing, I succeed in it. Life! What is life? A means—nothing but a means to bring about the triumph of one will. My will has triumphed. The first time I saw you I thought: "That woman shall either be my wife, or she shall be no man's." You found me always cold: if you had been able to plunge your hand into my heart, how soon you would have snatched it away from the intensity of the heat! But to-day no more of that. You will have it so, and I wrap myself round in ice once again. To-day no more: sleep, rest: to-morrow you shall answer me.

MAR. Answer! To what question?

PABLO. To this: "Why have you married me?" I shall wait till to-morrow.

MAR. I can answer you to-night.

PABLO. Then answer.

MAR. I have said it already : we women are not strong.   I wished to have by my side a strong being who should compel me to walk in the only path possible.

PABLO. The path of honour?

MAR. Of course.

PABLO. Then you will walk in it, and I suppose without my assistance.

MAR. And if I should need that assistance?

PABLO. I shall not fail you.

MAR. Under all its forms?

PABLO. Under all.

MAR. Even under the form of chastisement and vengeance?

PABLO (*advancing towards her*). Mariana !

MAR. Reply.   It is now my turn to question.

PABLO (*violently*). Then, under that form, too.

MAR. Indeed? (*Ironically.*)   And if you should not have the courage?

PABLO. Don't put me to the test.

MAR. If the case should happen I'll put you to it.

PABLO (*approaches her and takes her hand*). You are feverish ; lie down and rest.

MAR. To-morrow it may be I who shall request a complete explanation.

PABLO. I shall always be at your orders.

MAR. Adieu.

PABLO. Adieu. (*Stopping. Aside*). Ah ! Mariana, you don't know me.

MAR. To-morrow I shall know what this man is.
Exit PABLO.

MAR. (*listening*). Yes: he has gone into his room.   Ah ! I can breathe.   It seems as if, when he is at my side, . . . he robs me of the air.   To suffer . . . good : but one requires extension, space, the ambient atmosphere in which the suffering may expand itself. A confined sorrow is unendurable : it becomes condensed here (*Presses her forehead.*) and brings on madness. It becomes condensed here (*Pressing her bosom.*)—and the heart breaks. Now I am more calm. (*Goes to a window.*) How beautiful and how clear is the night! How the moon shines! (*Touches the bell, and* CLAUDIA *appears to the left with a lighted candle*). Tell them to come and take away those lights. That which you are now bringing will be enough for me. (*Takes it off her and puts it on a table. She afterwards takes off her travelling cloak and throws it upon the sofa.*)

CLAUD. Yes, señora. (*She goes out for an instant and returns with two male servants.*)

MAR. (*walking about nervously*). These people irritate me, and the light and the noise and all things are a trouble to me. (*To* CLAUDIA.) You may retire to rest. I shall go to bed alone.

CLAUD. If such is your order, señora. . . .

MAR. Yes : that is my order : and let my maid also go to bed.

CLAUD. A very good night, señora.

MAR. Good-night. (CLAUDIA *goes to shut the two windows in the back-centre.*) Don't shut those windows : so : as they are.

CLAUD. Yes, señora.

[*Exit. The male servants meanwhile take away the candelabra through the door to the left.*]

MAR. So : every one far from me. Alone—and thinking upon him. (*Approaches the table and puts out the light : the apartment remains illuminated by the moon alone ; in the first wing it is dark.*) Upon him . . . my eternal companion. (*Stops.*) Will he be thinking of me? Assuredly. With Daniel **there** can be no more than one idea—his Mariana, and the horrible treachery of his Mariana. Poor Daniel! Let him suffer, let him suffer, provided that he suffers for my sake: let him never console himself. Oh! that would be treachery indeed! (*Stopping.*) What noise is that? Is Pablo coming back? (*Goes to* PABLO'S *door and listens. Meanwhile the door of the private room of* MARIANA *opens, and* DANIEL *appears beyond the curtain: he comes with head uncovered and with dress rather disarranged, since it is understood that he has scrambled through the window. Meanwhile* MARIANA *listens close to the door of* PABLO: DANIEL *observes her*). Nothing is heard. He must be thinking of what he has to say to me to-morrow, and how he will make me tame. (*Bursts into suppressed laughter.*)

DAN. (*aside*). Wretch! wretch!   And she laughs and is merry! . . . Now I too shall be merry.

MAR. (*listening once more*). Everything is quiet. He will have locked himself in his room. I shall go to mine. (*Walking slowly.*) And my Daniel will be with me: always with Mariana: always. . . . (*Raises the curtain.*)

Enter DANIEL.

Ah! . . A man! What? Who is it? (*Retreating in terror.*)

DAN. (*following her*). Do you not recognise me now?

MAR. Daniel! . . . No! . . . A lie!   . Daniel!
(*The stage is illuminated only by the light of the moon, which flows in through the two great windows in the background, the same which, as has been said, were left open.*)

DAN. Don't run away. . . . Here!   Be calm!
. . . Silence! . . . (*Overtakes her and controls her.*)

MAR. Daniel! . . . Impossible! . . . It is a dream! . Leave me! Let me go . . . Daniel! . . . My God!

DAN. Be quiet! . . . Be quiet! . . . What,—did you think that on the night of your wedding day I could be far off?

MAR. But is it you? . . . Is it you?

DAN. You did not expect me—eh?

MAR. (*embracing him*). It is my Daniel! My Daniel! . . . It seems to me impossible!

DAN. And does my presence make you glad?

MAR. Don't you know it well? (*Passionately.*) Yes—it was right for you to be here!

DAN. But what kind of woman are you?

MAR. Mariana! (*Caressingly.*) It is you, now, who don't know me.

DAN. I don't know! . . . I shall go mad . . . and she looks upon me with fondness! . . . and almost strangles me in her arms! But the world is a crowd of mad-folk! And this woman—what is she? . . . Let me see . . . let me see . . . Come here . . . to the light . . . that I may look at you! (*Takes her to where the moonlight falls upon her.*)

MAR. Yes, look at me . . . look at me . . . and let me also look at you. . . . Now we have seen each other. . . . Now my heart has gathered up its treasure of joy for a long time to come. . . . And now, go away. . . . There, go away!

DAN. Already! . . . All those outbursts of passion were that I should go away! . . . I am the little lad to whom a toy is given . . . and they say to him: "Away with you: don't be troublesome." "Take a smile, Daniel: a caress: a fond phrase—and—be off, you disturb me." Well, I shall not go: that might have been long since. Now, (*fiercely*) I shall not go.

MAR. I wish it: I command it: it is imperative:
Go.

DAN. No: no: I tell you, no. It is I now who
shall give orders. (*Shaking her brutally.*)

MAR. Let go! Villain! If you don't go . . . I'll
call out.

DAN. To your husband?

MAR. To Pablo.

DAN. Where is he?

MAR. (*pointing to the room*).   There.

DAN. Her husband is tired of her already, and flies
from her!

MAR. You fool! . . . Don't you see that I have
suffered much to-day—that I thought I should have
gone mad! . . . I arrived here almost insensible.
I arrived ill . . . I begged him to leave me, . . .
and he went to his room.   All men are not cruel like
you.

DAN. You have suffered much to-day! (*With a
mixture of terror and joy.*)

MAR. Yes: more than you. You thought that
there could not be a sorrow more unbearable than
yours: well, yes there is: it is mine.

DAN. Then you don't love him!

MAR. Love him! . . . That man!   Poor
Daniel!

DAN. Then it is myself whom you love?

MAR. And if I answer that question, will you go?

DAN. Yes.

MAR. Swear it.

DAN. I swear it.

MAR. Then listen well: I only love one man:
yourself: Daniel: the Daniel that has possession of
my soul.   For you . . . I'd forfeit everything . . .
life itself!

DAN. Mariana ! . . . But all this is mockery : you are turning me into ridicule.

MAR. Making mockery of you !   No : I have loved you : I do love you : I shall love you for ever: I swear it to you by the memory of my mother.   So let that man come and deal out death to us both if I don't speak the truth.   You will not believe me, but God knows it : God believes me !   Go, Daniel: go: have pity on me and do not forget me !

DAN. The explanation of all this ! . . . Quick quick !

MAR. Never.   It is my secret.

DAN. No : I know you: you are deceiving me once more.   It would not be the first time : it would not be the second . . : but the last time has now gone by . . . Speak ! . . . Speak !

MAR. Go away.

DAN. No !

MAR. You swore you would

DAN. What do oaths matter to me—any more than they do to you?

MAR. Don't drive me mad.   Go away . . . or I shall call.

DAN. Well, then, I shall go.   (*Runs to the back and opens the door.*)

MAR. What are you doing?

DAN. Seeing that the way is clear.

MAR. What for?

DAN. That I may go out of this house.   I shall fulfil my word : I shall go out ; but not alone ; I mean to go with you.

MAR. No ! . . . That shall not be.

DAN. We two together : for ever !   I have forced the little door of the outer wall : a carriage is waiting for me : and in it we two .

MAR. (*retreating*). To where?

DAN. How do I know! Anywhere: where you please: where in all tranquillity you may love me, hate me, deceive me . . . but both together!

MAR. (*flying from him*).   No: I say no.

DAN. Yes ; I say yes.   (*Seizing her.*)

MAR. Let go, wretch ! . . . You have in you the blood of that wretched creature.

DAN. (*raising her forcibly*).   Well if you are obstinate, so shall I be. . . .

MAR. Let go . . . keep off. . . .   I despise you . . . I hate you! . . . Monster! . . . Villain! . . . No . . . no . . . You shall not do with me what Alvarado did with my mother! (*Beside herself: maddened by the struggle : not knowing what she says.*)

DAN. What? . . . What does this woman say? . . . (*Setting her down : she flies from him, stands apart and gazes at him triumphantly.*)

MAR. That! . . . That !   What I have told you! . . . You now see that you shall not bear me away !

DAN. Alvarado !   Who is Alvarado ? . . . Was it my father?

MAR. Yes! . . . (*In another tone : a tone of supreme sorrow.*)

DAN. (*with horrible anguish*).   And your mother? . Is that what I am to understand?

MAR. Yes !

DAN. And he? . . . And she? . . . Then it was for that?

MAR. For that !

DAN. For that you have hated me?

MAR. I ought to have hated you. . . . Yes. . . . Hate you ! . . . And I love you with all my soul;

what more can you ask? . . . (*At a distance, in anguish, with weeping, in a low voice. A solemn but not too prolonged pause.*)

DAN. My God! . . . My God! . . . Mariana! Mariana! . . . one word—no more . . . may I ask you to forgive me? . . .

MAR. Forgive you, poor Daniel? For what?

DAN. And will you continue to love me? (*Approaching her.*)

MAR. For ever!

DAN. (*still closer*). And you will forget all?

MAR. All.—But forget you?—No: not that. You I shall never forget. (*Approaching him as if magnetised.*)

DAN. And when all that's forgotten, you have no past, neither have I. (*Close to her; in a sweet and tempting voice.*) We are two beings who meet, who become united, who shall not now be separated. (*Clasping her round the waist.*) And we two shall go alone thus through the world! We shall see before us a most beautiful garden. . . . Then . . . we have but to cross it . . . Mariana! . . . Mariana! . . . My only possession! . . . My life! . . . Am I not the being whom you most love in creation? Then what does the rest of creation matter to you? You are with me! Are not you all that exists in my eyes? Then what does anything else matter to me? I am with you. Poor woman, poor Mariana, poor little sufferer in imagination! Make a sacrifice of illusions, phantoms, remembrances; come to a living, present, palpitating happiness. Do you love me? Do I love you? Then let all the rest vanish and pass away like a ridiculous masquerade. Look around you and you will see nothing more than your Daniel, and your moving shadow commingled with mine, and a very

bright moon which paints in white for our sake a
pathway of that garden which conducts to liberty, to
happiness, to love, to delirium, to heaven! Because
for us alone, if you have courage, God has created
heaven.—Come, Mariana.

MAR. Daniel!   I can no more ... my strength
is failing me ... my head whirls round ... my
heart leaps from me ... there run through my body
cold shudderings that shake me to pieces! ... My
God! ... My God! ... Have compassion on me!
I love you, I love you, Daniel, most dearly! (*Now
conquered.*)

DAN. Poor Mariana, you are trembling with cold.
It is the faint breeze of the coming morn. . . . When
inside my carriage I shall wrap you up well. .
Look ... look ... here you have left your travelling
cloak. (*Picking up the one which was left on a chair.*)
I shall help you ... my Mariana. . . . (*Putting the
cloak on her.*) Quick ... make haste ... let us
go. . . . Am I not helping you? ... My Mariana.
. . . My own Mariana. . . . You now see whether I
love you. . . . I am helping you as if you were a little
child. . . . The little child of my soul! ... My own
little child! (*This awakens the memory of* MARIANA
*to that part of her life described in the Second
Act.*)

MAR. (*utters a scream and tears herself away from*
DANIEL). It was in this way my mother dressed me
that night! ... No ... let go ... Pablo! .
(*Dashing herself against the door of her husband's
room.*) Pablo! ... Pablo! ... Come—for I am
an infamous woman! . . .

DAN. Madwoman, what are you doing?

MAR. Now you shall see! ... Pablo, help! ...
Your honour calls you! . . .

DAN. Do you then hate me? Do you not love your Daniel?

MAR. You shall now see whether I love you. . . . Pablo! . . . Come to me! . . . to your vile wife! . . To me! . . .

Enter PABLO *with a revolver in his hand. Still the light of the moon alone.*

PABLO. Who calls? What's this? Mariana ! A man!

MAR. It is Daniel! . . . (*Pointing to* DANIEL *and embracing him.*)

PABLO (*to* DANIEL). Wretch!

DAN. Wretch yourself, who have robbed me of what was mine.

MAR. We are both wretches. (*Pointing to herself and* DANIEL.) Listen! I always loved him. I married you through jealousy! . . . I was going to run away with him. Do you understand? If you let me go, I shall run away. Let us see what you will do. It is now your turn. What will you do? What will you do, Pablo? I love him. What will you do? (*Still in the embrace of* DANIEL *as if challenging* DON PABLO.)

PABLO. That which you desired of me! . . . (*Fires upon* MARIANA *who reels to the ground.*)

DAN. Mariana! . . (*Throwing himself upon her.*) Mariana! . . . Mariana! . . . My darling! Answer me! . . . Mariana!

PABLO. I am waiting for you! . . .

DAN. That's true! (*Arising with a terrible look.*) This man still remains to me!

PABLO. Are you armed?

DAN. Yes. (*Drawing, or pointing to where he has, a revolver.*)

PABLO. Then let us go there. (*Indicating the garden.*)

DAN. Let us go.

PABLO. It shall now be a combat of life and death.

DAN. There was only one life that was worth combating for; and that lies there. (*Pointing to the body of* MARIANA.) What matters for such lives as ours ! . . . Adieu ! . . . No ! . . . I shall be with you soon, Mariana ! I shall be with you soon !

[*Exeunt towards the garden.*

END OF THE DRAMA.

The Gresham Press,
UNWIN BROTHERS
CHILWORTH AND LONDON.

CPSIA information can be obtained at www.ICGtesting.com
Printed in the USA
LVOW10s2016080716

495571LV00030B/184/P